ADVANCE PRAISE FOR *AFRICAN AMERICANS IN INDIANAPOLIS*

"The story of the Black experience in Indianapolis is one of hardship, triumph, and hope. As we continue to write that story, it's vital to know where we've been. David Leander Williams expertly explores and examines that rich history in his new book. As a native Hoosier and a proud Black man, I am continually inspired by our ancestors who helped build our city and make it a more just and equitable community. Mr. Williams is giving these heroes and sheroes the credit they are due, and for that I am grateful."

—Representative Andre Carson, US Congressman,
Seventh District of Indiana

"Once again, David is filling in the blank pages of a history that has been intentionally excluded, diluted, diminished. This book must be placed in libraries and classrooms throughout the city, state, and country so teachers, parents, and children—all children—will learn the authentic truth about the unrelenting trials and tribulations faced by a people who refused to allow systemic racism to break their spirit and dismantle their goals. The story of *African Americans in Indianapolis* during the period of 1820 to 1970 is but a microcosm of our story wherever we are or have been. Dr. John Henrik Clarke, noted professor and historian, tells us that 'to control a people you must first control what they think about themselves and how they regard their history and culture. And when your conqueror makes you ashamed of your culture and your history, he needs no prison walls and no chains to hold you.' David Leander Williams, we are so grateful that your brilliance was molded, shaped, and developed by the extraordinary professors at Crispus Attucks High School, and now it's being illuminated and used to benefit your people and all others whose lives this book will touch. The Ancestors are smiling."

—Patricia Payne, Director, Racial Equity Office,
Indianapolis Public Schools

"Without a doubt, David Leander Williams has saved the day. For all of the people who have contributed stories about Black life in Indianapolis, Mr. Williams has picked up the pieces and formed them into this deep perspective of African American history in the Hoosier capitol. Unlike other local histories, *African Americans in Indianapolis* pays homage to national, political, and social issues that have affected Indianapolis. It is destined to become a staple not only on bookshelves in Indiana but on bookshelves of history lovers everywhere."

—Stanley Warren, DePauw University

AFRICAN
AMERICANS
IN
INDIANAPOLIS

AFRICAN AMERICANS IN INDIANAPOLIS

The Story of a People Determined to Be Free

DAVID LEANDER WILLIAMS

INDIANA UNIVERSITY PRESS

This book is a publication of

Indiana University Press
Office of Scholarly Publishing
Herman B Wells Library 350
1320 East 10th Street
Bloomington, Indiana 47405 USA

iupress.org

Manufactured in the United States of America

First printing 2022

Cataloging information is available from the Library of Congress.

ISBN 978-0-253-05948-2 (hardback)
ISBN 978-0-253-05949-9 (paperback)
ISBN 978-0-253-05950-5 (ebook)

TO. Jim & Nicole
This book was inspired
by my association

Dedicated to the baby boomers, millennials,
Generation X, and Generation Z of all races, creeds, and
colors who strive toward freedom, justice, equality,
and empowerment in search of
a more perfect union.

with Tedd as a civil
Rights worker back in
the day of th' Turbulent 60s
Dr. King, Malcolm X, Bobby Kennedy
Viet Nam War etc he fought
to make a change and
succeeded!!! We waz
"crazy" but determined!!!
Best

CONTENTS

PREFACE

THE GENESIS OF THE PUBLICATION of this book occurred two decades ago when my bewildered niece wandered into my computer room, with a look of anguish accentuated by anxiety written across her cherubic face. She had been charged by her social studies teacher with the task of writing short biographical sketches of local African American trailblazers and history makers or significant events that occurred in Indianapolis during the nineteenth and twentieth centuries. She lamented, in her young mind, the notion that many of the Black history projects she had completed in the past, during Black History Month, centered on old, dark, moldy, shadowy figures like Harriet Tubman, Sojourner Truth, William Edward Burghardt DuBois, Rosa Parks, or Dr. Martin Luther King Jr. They lived in the dark, dank basements of libraries and historical societies and were resuscitated in February of each year, trotted out to an adoring public, and returned to their dungeons on the first day of March.

I reflected on my educational experience at the segregated Crispus Attucks High School and identified with her disillusionment. I remember our school celebrating Negro History Week, wherein the photographs and biographies of several African American history makers like Frederick Douglass, Ida B. Wells, and Mary McLeod Bethune adorned the space above the blackboards, but only for one week. This history was not incorporated into our curriculum, and I never saw these figures' photos in our textbooks or class assignments. Interestingly, we had permanent photographs of Presidents George Washington and Abraham Lincoln and explorer Christopher Columbus, who purportedly discovered America and the Native Americans, who had inhabited this land thousands of years before his ship sailed from Spain in 1492.

I understood my niece's concern and inability to grasp the history or identify with our heroes of yesteryear, many of whom lived and died centuries ago. I took her by the hand, and we walked to the Indianapolis Central Library to begin our historical exploration. After an hour of searching many collections, we were totally exhausted and comically thought of the nursery rhyme of "Ole Mother Hubbard who went to the cupboard to give her poor dog a bone; when she came there, the cupboard was bare, and so the poor dog had none." There was not one book, adult or juvenile, that dealt comprehensively with the history of African Americans in Indianapolis!

We traveled to the Crispus Attucks High School to consult with educators and discovered that in 1938 a distinguished social studies teacher, Dr. Joseph Cephas Carroll, wrote *Slave Insurrections in the United States: 1800–1865*, which was based on his doctoral dissertation from the Ohio State University. Decades later, another distinguished Crispus Attucks social studies teacher, Dr. Stanley Warren, wrote *Crispus Attucks High School: Hail to the Green, Hail to the Gold* and *The Senate Avenue Y. M. C. A. for African-American Men and Boys*.

We visited the Butler University library and discovered two books by Professor Emma Lou Thornbrough, *This Far by Faith: Black Hoosier Heritage* and *The Negro in Indiana before 1900: A Study of a Minority*. Afterward, we traveled to the Indiana Historical Society and discovered the book authored by Dr. Richard B. Pierce, *Polite Protest: The Political Economy in Indianapolis, 1920–1970*. Finally, we discovered fine works by individuals who had interesting connections to Indiana Avenue history. A'Lelia Bundles, the great-granddaughter of Madam C. J. Walker, wrote *On Her Own Ground: The Life and Times of Madam C. J. Walker* and *Madam Walker Theatre Center: An Indianapolis Treasure*. Thomas Howard Ridley Jr., an Indiana Avenue resident and nonagenarian who is considered the dean of Indiana Avenue history, wrote *From the Avenue: A Memoir*. Hoosier author Phillip Hoose wrote *Hoosiers: The Fabulous Basketball Life of Indiana* and *Attucks! Oscar Robertson and the Basketball Team That Awakened a City*. These historical masterpieces covered important periods in the history of African Americans in Indianapolis and aided me immensely in my research and documentation. However, I wanted to take a more comprehensive, panoramic snapshot of that history to illustrate the historical connectivity between these periods and their relationship to contemporary issues. For example, how did the rights and privileges stipulated in the Emancipation Proclamation influence the treatment of African Americans in Indianapolis in the early twentieth century? Did the sacrifices of African American soldiers in the Spanish-American War and World War II contribute to the empowerment of Blacks in Indianapolis in later decades?

Further, I opined that in this period in the twenty-first century, with the issues and sentiments swirling around and dividing the country—systematic institutional racism; anti-Black, anti-Mexican, anti-Hispanic, antisemitic, anti-African, anti-Muslim, anti-immigrant, and anti-gay and lesbian sentiments; voter suppression; and reparations—being hotly debated in legislatures across the nation, the history of the vestiges of the "Original Sin," slavery, should be dissected and discussed. How can we possibly begin to solve these long-lasting problems and deal with their resolutions honestly if we have not examined the *history* of African Americans in Indianapolis?

I also realized that many young, inquiring, ambitious students may have had the fire of inquiry and exploration extinguished in their young minds by this gross omission. Many may have believed that the lack of prominent historical personalities of color in their textbooks indicates that individuals who looked like them did not make significant contributions to the fabric of Indianapolis history and did not deserve one dot of printer's ink. Perhaps these feelings of anomie or historical rejection may later have had an adverse impact on their quest for knowledge and positive feelings of pride and importance. Perhaps this omission might have affected their desire to compete academically and had a devastating effect on future standardized test scores.

For weeks and weeks, I complained that somebody should do something about this travesty of history! We have a rich historical and cultural heritage that must be documented and recorded, and only a few books have been written to underscore this factor. I surmised that personalities of color have made outstanding contributions to Indianapolis history and certainly should be honored. I regretfully realized that the faces of many of these people had long been hidden away in dusty family albums in attics or lost to the fading memories of the elderly. Somebody will have to answer to future generations as to why the African Americans of the late twentieth century did not recognize the value of our history for not only Indianapolis but the world. How can we chart our course for the future if we know very little about our past? Early one morning as I walked into the den, I glanced at my mirror and saw that "somebody" whom I had previously railed against sardonically smiling back at me. It was me! I must do something!

I immediately understood that we must ask many questions if we are to evaluate our journey from the founding of Indianapolis in 1820 to the present day. What historical challenges did downtrodden people of color overcome in their struggle to gain their freedom and equality? What historical events served as trail markers on Indianapolis African Americans' march toward independence? Can we learn from these milestones and chart a course for the twenty-first century? Were all segments of the majority community determined to impede African American progress during this period? Did segments of the majority community fight racism and discrimination and aid African Americans in their march toward freedom? Can African Americans' historical strides toward freedom point to the racial progress and equity that may be achieved in the twenty-first century?

I was transported to the shores near Port Comfort, Virginia, in August 1619—a year before the historic landing of the *Mayflower* and its pilgrims at Plymouth Rock—when the *Dutch Man of War* dropped its anchor in Jamestown, Virginia, and seventeen emaciated Africans disembarked. This was the genesis of African American history in the New World. I was mindful of the fact that a span of a little more than two hundred years separated this historic event from the birth of Indianapolis in 1820. I wanted to examine the important milestones in Indianapolis history that may have been connected to the plight of those innocent African slaves who departed that ship in Virginia. I wanted to observe the evolution of human history for better or for worse and wanted desperately to make sure that the rich, extraordinary history of African Americans in Indianapolis was documented and celebrated. Thus, I embarked on my journey through two centuries of Indianapolis African American history to find and to polish these invaluable and sometimes painful gems of our existence. I hurried to the Indiana Historical Society, Indiana State Library, and Crispus Attucks Museum archives to begin my research. I read every African American newspaper from the 1880s to 1970 and discovered numerous stories that had been omitted from history textbooks. Why was this knowledge hidden? Was the history so disheartening that one should not recognize its impact? Should we omit this precious history and hope that it would eventually fade away? Should we not embrace this history in the hope that it might reveal strategies to solve contemporary issues? These and other questions swirled through my mind.

Indianapolis must understand that to battle racism, one must hold honest, sober discussions. Racism may never be completely eradicated in Indianapolis, but it can be contained first by a sincere apology for misdeeds of the past and a genuine dialogue among honest people who seek a more just society. The history of every segment of society must be documented, recorded, and respected. I realize that the publication of this book will not be the proverbial silver bullet to destroy all the racial and social problems addressed within this work; however, if it can provide a few grains of gunpowder, then my humble, sincere effort will not have been in vain.

According to an old Ghanaian proverb "the tree that has poisoned roots bears unhealthy fruit"—a clarion call to those who seek justice that was echoed decades ago in Lerone Bennett Jr.'s masterpiece of African American history, *Before the Mayflower*. He writes that there is a regrettable tendency in some circles to regard Black history as an intellectual ghetto. Worse yet, some people regard it as a minor-league pastime involving the recitation of dates and the names of Black greats. But Black history read right is a much more fateful encounter than that. Read right, within the context of social forces struggling for dominance, the history detailed on these pages raises questions about the destiny of America and the orientation of our lives. It is on this deep level, and within this context, that we are invited to understand a perceptive remark by African American author Ralph Ellison, who said once, in another connection, that "the end is in the beginning, and lies far ahead."

ACKNOWLEDGMENTS

I AM GREATLY INDEBTED TO the late Wilma Gibbs-Moore, senior archivist for African American history, Indiana Historical Society; Ethel Milligan-Middlebrook, researcher and historical consultant; Dr. Stanley Warren, professor emeritus, DePauw University; Dr. H. Rose Adesiyan, professor emerita, Purdue University, Calumet; Frances Glenn-Jennings, historian/musicologist; Ted Green, documentarian; Dr. Patricia Payne, coordinator, Crispus Attucks Racial Equity Office; Annmarie Amor Byers, education consultant, Crispus Attucks Racial Equity Office; the financial contribution of Bruce Buchanan; Flanner and Buchanan Inc.; Laura Williams-Town, publishing consultant; Suzanne Hahn, Indiana Historical Society, vice president of archives and library; Dorothy Springs, education specialist/life coach; Guenet Aster Williams, computer specialist; Thedora E Lewis, educator; Deacon J. C. Ward, Mount Olive Baptist Church; Brother Homer Chappel, Mount Olive Baptist Church; Ruth Waller-Chappel, Mount Olive Baptist Church; Sister Geraldine Hawkins, Mount Olive Baptist Church; Rodney Walker, graphic artist; Shonna Jennings, graphic artist; Iyassu Chernet, musicologist/historian; Cassandra Williams, clinical faculty, Africana Studies, Indiana University–Purdue University at Indianapolis; Lorna Dawe, events and communication coordinator, Indiana University–Purdue University at Indianapolis; Michael Robbins, jazz historian; Nina Shirley-McCoy, Lockefield historian/artist; Gerald Hause, Lockefield historian; Mike Perkins, public service librarian, the Indianapolis Public Library; Jordan Hunt, public service librarian, the Indianapolis Public Library; Thomas Probasco, public service librarian, the Indianapolis Public Library; the late John Dumas-Haamid; Rosalind Dumas-Haamid; Kenney Adams; Carole Adams; Harold Andrews; Freida Andrews; Waller Chappel; Martha Chappel; Henry

Woods; Ruth Woods; Lockefield Civic Association; Darlene Levy, formerly of Indiana State Library; Fred Robinson, Crispus Attucks Alumni Association; Pamela Hurley-Shultz, computer specialist, London, Kentucky; Winford Cork, jazz historian; Woodie Carpenter, jazz historian; Thomas Ridley; Nancy Holliman-Johnson; Indiana Avenue historians Fred Taylor and Frazier King; Olivia McGee-Lockhart, Crispus Attucks History Club; Dorothea Embry-Whitfield; Andrew Ramsey; Louise Smith; Dennis Nichols; Eunice Trotter; Mary Ruth Bernard-Black; Godfrey Muhammad; Cezar Allen Williams; Tate Matthew Williams; and Sandra Yvonne Wright. Their contributions to the success of this book are immeasurable, and I sincerely appreciate their generosity and professionalism.

AFRICAN
AMERICANS
IN
INDIANAPOLIS

—ʍ—

INDIANA BECOMES A STATE

THE YEAR 2020 WAS THE bicentennial celebration of the history of Indianapolis. During this yearlong celebration, numerous segments of our population
glanced back to the bygone days that began in the early settlement of Vincennes,
Indiana. They asked questions as to what role the African American community
played in the evolution of Indianapolis and its journey toward progress and
tranquility: Were their contributions significant, and were they recognized and
justly documented by future historians? How might future generations make
the connection between the battles waged during previous centuries and the
social circumstances faced today?

Some Indianapolis communities faced daunting circumstances such as abject poverty, disease, and hunger that impeded their journey toward freedom.
Nevertheless, they persevered and struggled tirelessly to improve their stations
in life. The African American community in particular encountered additional
obstacles but used them as points of inspiration that empowered them to succeed. Because they were marginalized by the additional factor of race, their
journey took a considerably different, more serpentine course, replete with
chuckholes and dead-end signs that other Hoosiers could only imagine.

As African Americans ponder the road traveled during the past two centuries, we must ask which events were important to overcome to mitigate the
plight of our people. How did we, as former slaves who were considered three-
fifths of a human being (according to article 1, section 2 of the US Constitution
of 1787, in reference to the House of Representatives' proportional representation scheme), survive and prosper?

What historical events over this two-hundred-year period served as genera-
tional markers that indicated changes, for better or for worse, in our existence?

Were we able to struggle alone, or did the majority community who championed our plight offer assistance? How did we deal with atrocities that were committed against us? Did some of the disastrous episodes of our struggle empower us to fight even harder and to shed the shackles of our lowly existence? How did local, national, and international events affect our community?

How did we combat the social problems that resulted from our history of slavery? How did we embrace education as a vehicle for a better life in Indianapolis? What was the racial climate of America in other ethnic communities and the severity of problems encountered in Indianapolis? What role did the church play in the struggle of African Americans in Indianapolis? What measures did African Americans take to assure majority Americans of their worthiness to be bona fide American citizens?

It will be necessary to examine the various episodes in Indianapolis African American history from 1820 to 1970 and highlight the battles that were waged for racial equality. Perhaps, with what we learn from this analysis, we can chart our course for a continued struggle for future decades. It will be of paramount importance to visit various episodes of African American history and see how they are connected to the struggle that we encounter today. We shall examine the relationship between various institutions and individuals of many colors who played a role in this evolution. We hope to examine the dynamics of racial oppression during this period and compare them with other regions of America that face this dilemma.

Hopefully, we can examine the historical dynamics of this period and clearly understand the trials and tribulations African Americans endured during this march to freedom.

At the dawn of the nineteenth century, several events in Indiana history served as a harbinger of future episodes that magnified African Americans' struggle against slavery and indentured servitude. These events clearly demonstrated the will and resolve of African Americans; although tethered by the chains of oppression, they were determined to strive against all odds and be free. Polly Strong and Mary Bateman-Clark were obviously not familiar with the inner machinations of the sophisticated and complicated legal system that kept them in bondage. Nevertheless, they stepped into the legal arena, with the assistance of a dedicated white attorney, and battled fiercely for their freedom. The historical accounts of these two ladies of color provide an example of the unyielding and uncompromising determination that African Americans would exhibit in future decades.[1]

The early history of Indiana can be traced to the southwestern part of the state where the city of Vincennes is now located. The city was founded in 1732 by French fur traders and was named in honor of Lieutenant and Commandant of Southern Indiana Francois-Marie Bissot, Sieur de Vincennes, who was also known by the anglicized appellation of Francis Morgan De Vincennes. In May 1722, he was commissioned an ensign and took control of Fort Ouiatenon, near present-day Lafayette, Indiana. He was promoted to the rank of lieutenant in 1730 and was made commandant to what is now southern Indiana. On March 25, 1736, Vincennes was burned at the stake along with other French captives by the indigenous Chickasaw Nation at the village of Ogula Tchetoka, near present-day Fulton, Mississippi. In 1746, a settlement called Vincennes was established on the banks of the Wabash River. It included four citizens and five slaves. The French instituted "Black Codes" of conduct that dictated protocol and regulated the daily activities of slaves, and they included the compulsory conversion to Roman Catholicism. Slaves were considered to be property with the commensurate value of livestock.[2]

During this period, intermarriage took place between the French fur traders and Native Americans. During the old French period, Cardinals Drouet and Vaudry and the Jesuits owned Black slaves. Such slaves were brought to Post Vincennes by the settlers of the "slave states."[3]

After the conclusion of the American Revolutionary War (1775–1783), in which Americans aided by the French defeated the British in a war over unfair tax policies, the British were routed but slavery remained as an institution of the former government. On July 13, 1787, the US Congress passed the Northwest Ordinance, which established a government for the area north and west of the Ohio River, which included Indiana.

A provision in the ordinance specifically stated: "There shall be neither slavery nor involuntary servitude in said territory, otherwise than in the punishment of crimes, whereof the party shall have been duly convicted: provided always, that any person escaping into the same, from whom labor or services is lawfully claimed in any one of the original states, such fugitive may be lawfully reclaimed and conveyed to the person claiming his or her labor or service, as foresaid."[4] Although an antislavery sentiment existed in the territory, there were citizens who owned slaves and fought tirelessly to overturn and abolish this provision. Many reasoned that the abolition of slavery and the freeing of their slaves would threaten their livelihood and way of life and simultaneously deal them a fatal economic blow. Therefore, they had to devise a strategy to challenge the legality of this provision. After careful examination of the articles of the Northwest Ordinance, they discovered a loophole in the provision. It did not succinctly specify the status of those who were slaves before the Northwest Ordinance was enacted, and this factor could serve as a basis for an appeal. The first governor of Indiana, William Henry Harrison, whose father and grandfather owned forty slaves in Virginia, crafted legislation referring to indentured servitude. It was nothing more than a subterfuge to subvert the provision whereby a slave could be brought to Indiana and freed and then required by his master to agree to be an indentured servant for a specified number of years. If the slave refused, then he or she could immediately be returned to slavery.[5] On this basis, two highly publicized court cases emerged that forever challenged the question of indentured servitude and slavery in Indiana.

Mary Bateman-Clark (fig. 1.1) was born a slave in Kentucky in 1795. In 1814, she was purchased by Benjamin J. Harrison in Kentucky as a slave for life. In 1815, Harrison transported her to the Indiana Territory, in what would later be called Vincennes, Indiana, and indentured her to himself for thirty years. On October 24, 1816, he sold her to General Washington Johnston for $300, whereupon she was forced to agree to work for twenty years. Bateman-Clark had no other alternative than to sign this agreement. In a suit filed years later, she was freed from this contract.[6]

In May 1816, the US Congress gave the Indiana Territory permission to form a government and join the union as the state of Indiana. The dilemma in reference to indentured servitude and slavery relative to the Northwest Ordinance would later be adjudicated and resolved after the consideration of the case of Polly Strong, a contemporary of Mary Bateman-Clark.

Polly Strong (fig. 1.2) was born in 1794 and was a slave owned by Hyacinthe Laselle, a prominent businessman well respected in his community. Because Strong's mother, Jenny, was a slave, many slave owners independently determined that she and her brother, James, were slaves and sentenced them to involuntary servitude for life. Many petitions were filed against this determination, but none were successful. During this period, Amory Kinney, an attorney, migrated from upstate New York to Vincennes and set up his law practice. Immediately it became apparent that he held deep antislavery convictions, and when made aware of the legal dynamics of the Bateman-Clark and Strong cases, he set into motion a gallant attempt to challenge these injustices.[7]

The Knox County Lower Court judges agreed that since Strong was the daughter of a slave, then she should be considered a slave for life, without any prospect of freedom. On May 12, 1820, Kinney filed appeals in the Indiana Supreme Court, with the cases of Bateman-Clark and Strong considered separately. The Supreme Court of Judicature of the State of Indiana at Corydon, the state capitol, in November 1821 ruled, "A free woman of color above 21 years of age bound herself by indenture in this State, for a valuable consideration, to serve the oblige as a menial servant for 20 years: Held, that a specific performance of

Fig.1.1 and 1.2 Mary Bateman-Clark and Polly Strong of Vincennes, Indiana. They fought for their freedom. Drawing by Shonna Jennings.

the contract could not be enforced; and that, upon a writ of habeas corpus, she had a right to be discharged from custody." Strong's appeal was adjudicated, and it was overturned on the basis of the applicability of the Northwest Ordinance. Clark's case was adjudicated and reversed, and the court ruled that personal services could not be forced. The three judges, Isaac Blackford, Jesse Holman, and James Scott, reversed the Knox County Lower Court decision. Mary Bateman-Clark and Polly Strong were free.[8]

According to some histories, the earliest Black person to enter the area that became the city of Indianapolis was Aaron Wallace, the young male servant of General John Tipton. The general brought Wallace to the area when Tipton was helping to select the site of Indianapolis as the state capital in 1820. However, Wallace did not establish a permanent residency. Historically, the first Black

Fig. 1.3 Pastoral scene of early Indianapolis, White River banks, circa 1820. Drawing by Shonna Jennings.

resident of Indianapolis was Cheney Lively, who was the housekeeper for Alexander Ralston, one of the founders of Indianapolis. She arrived in Indianapolis in 1820. After Ralston's death on January 5, 1827, Lively remained in the city and lived on property that she owned on Maryland Street. Also in 1820, Dr. S. G. Mitchell, the city's earliest doctor, brought another Black person to Indianapolis, Ephraim Ensaw, a freedman who worked for wages. By 1821, other Blacks had settled in the city, including David Mallory, the city's first barber. By 1836, Indianapolis Blacks were clustered on the banks of the White River in an area later called Bucktown (fig. 1.3), Sleigho, or Colored Town.[9]

It would be a gross understatement to say that Indiana in the nineteenth century was hospitable to its African American citizenry, as evidenced by the later adoption of article 13 of the 1851 state constitution. This article decreed that "no Negro or mulatto shall come into or settle in the state."[10] This act was obviously designed to impede the influx of fugitive slaves who might flee to the state after an escape or of free Blacks, after emancipation. Free African Americans and Quakers welcomed them and even constructed an Underground Railroad to facilitate their escape from slavery, but many white Indiana residents were violently opposed to the migration of Blacks into the state. They feared that the influx of Blacks into the manual labor market would result in employment disaster for poor whites and a fatal blow to their economy.

If there was any question as to whether the climate of social change and acceptance of African Americans in Indiana had improved a few decades after the Mary Bateman-Clark and Polly Strong cases, there were several cases in Indianapolis and New Albany that would serve as barometers of the politics of the day.

EARLY INDIANAPOLIS

DURING THE EARLY NINETEENTH CENTURY in Indianapolis, no one collected demographic data regarding income, education, socioeconomic class, employment, and migration patterns of African Americans. This data would not be available until more than a century and a half later. The earliest documentation of African Americans in Indianapolis was gleaned from family Bibles and oral histories. Unfortunately, this insufficient information could not provide a clear view of the early community that developed on the banks of the White River. Most of the time local newspapers did not include information on African Americans in their mentions of various racial or ethnic groups. This omission was due to three factors: the stifling racial climate of the day; the fact that slavery was one of the most prominent economic institutions of this period; and many community members' belief that African Americans were chattel and not worthy of documentation.

In 1821, a tragic event changed the demographics of the area, having an effect that would last for decades. Before that year, many shanties and dilapidated structures dotted the landscape near the White River, in the area where Indiana Avenue would later be constructed. In 1821, a catastrophic flood sent water over the banks of the White River and caused substantial loss of life and considerable property damage. The strong currents washed away both shanties and livestock. Water flooded much of the low-lying area where poor German and Irish settlers lived, and the resulting drainage problem created stagnant pools and a rancid odor. As mosquitoes bred and hatched in these pools, a malaria outbreak occurred. As settlers died, word spread that the banks of the river were the breeding ground of disease, and the White River acquired the name of the "River of Death." Frantically, almost every white family with the economic capacity to relocate took their meager belongings and moved to higher and drier grounds. This white flight left the fertile but disease-infested land available.

As recently migrated African Americans (many of whom were escaped slaves from the South) arrived in Indianapolis, they viewed the vacant land as immediately available real estate and either built shanties or occupied the housing of the fleeing German and Irish settlers.[1]

It is highly conceivable that as more African Americans migrated to Indianapolis and settled on the banks of the White River, others questioned the move and sought alternative housing possibilities. Some more economically stable Black families may have opted to secure housing on higher ground adjacent to Indiana Avenue for fear of another flood and malarial outbreak. As the availability of housing declined and the prospects of inclement weather increased, Blacks began to construct small shanties and inhabit dilapidated shacks on Indiana Avenue.[2]

In 1836, Augustus Turner, a Black barber, met with a group of people in his log cabin home that also doubled as a barbershop, at 67 West Georgia Street. The Black community felt that its spiritual needs were being ignored and that this vital concern needed to be addressed. Turner may have received information from other religious communities in neighboring states that the AME church of Philadelphia was rapidly expanding and establishing churches throughout the country. There, in Turner's modest dwelling, the dream of Bethel African Methodist Episcopal church was first envisioned. After much prayer, soul-searching, and serious meditation, the elders of the community took steps to make their dream of a church for the African American community become a reality.

The Reverend William Paul Quinn was the first religious leader to serve the church. Quinn was the son of an Indian mahogany merchant and an African woman and religious leader who supported his calling to the pulpit. He converted from Hinduism to Christianity over his father's objections. He was an AME circuit preacher commissioned by the Philadelphia Conference of the AME church. He traveled the winding, dusty roads of Pennsylvania, West Virginia, and Ohio to spread the Gospel and establish new churches. Arriving in Indiana on horseback in 1836, he established Bethel AME church in Richmond, Indiana. Later that year, he rode west to Indianapolis and established the Indianapolis Station, later called Vermont Street AME church and ultimately known as Bethel AME church (fig. 2.1).

In addition to serving the spiritual needs of the newly established Black community, Bethel AME church provided the political glue that held that community together. Many forums and community meetings took place in the church, and it provided a welcome station for many recently arrived Blacks. In

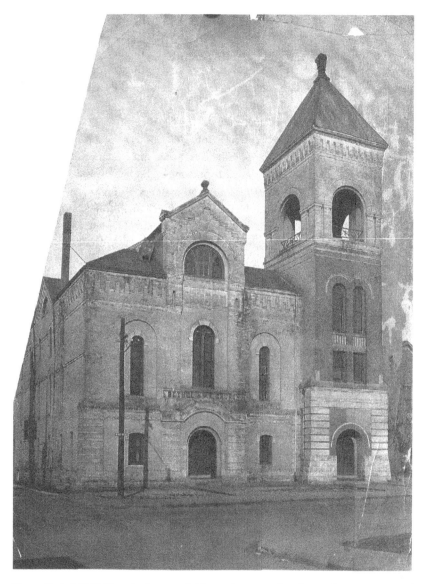

Fig. 2.1 Bethel AME Church, the second African American church in Indiana. Courtesy of Indiana Historical Society.

the middle of the nineteenth century, while abolitionists were spiriting slaves from southern plantations to freedom in the north, they sought guidance from Black settlers who worshipped at Bethel AME. Also, they helped shelter Black travelers who either decided to remain in Indianapolis or journey to northern territories, including Canada. Blacks organized their community and adopted strategies to improve their stations in life. They pondered questions as to how they could strive toward freedom and not be a threat to the community and harness the powers of the church to aid them in their journey toward freedom. They also wondered how they might comport themselves spiritually, socially, and economically and gain the respect of the majority community.

Obviously, church members were warned not to reveal the Underground Railroad activities for fear that they would jeopardize the safety of both the slaves and, more importantly, the pastor. A distinct anti-abolitionist tenor permeated the atmosphere in the majority community, as evidenced by the reports of brutal attacks on African Americans throughout the city. Reportedly, many escaped slaves left at night for destinations farther north—even as far as Canada, where their safety was assured.

African Americans who migrated to Indianapolis shortly after the founding of Bethel AME are believed to have lived in a community north of the Central Canal, south of Fall Creek, and west of the White River, in the area that would later become Indiana Avenue. There, they inherited a community emptied by fears of malaria, a place where they might have some degree of protection thanks to the generosity of a tiny mosquito.[3]

A decade later, residents of this community gave themselves the questionable name of Bucktown. There has been a continual debate as to the origin of the name. Two theories predominate. The first is that racist whites selected the name because the area was predominantly inhabited by Blacks and because it was common pejorative parlance to refer to a Black male as a buck. Many expressions such as *buck dance* and *Black buck* were used to stereotype Blacks during this period. This stereotypical caricature was a barefooted Black man with white lips and bright eyes who was obediently docile to the point of being infantile. Books and minstrel songs of this period were replete with references to the Black buck and his buffoonish behavior.

The second theory, which has more credibility, is that this community derived its name from the antics of a group of white construction workers. Newspaper accounts reveal that a group of roving laborers arrived in Indianapolis as part of the workforce that was contracted to construct the National Road (also known as Cumberland Road), at what is present-day Washington Street and US Highway 40. These men were not considered model citizens. They snatched chickens from the backyards of small shanties, stole vegetables from gardens, robbed people in broad daylight, and engaged in drunken and boisterous activities during all hours of the day and night. According to early Indiana historian Jacob Piatt, "The pariah of early Indianapolis was a man named David Burkhardt, who called his followers the 'chain gang.'" He settled in the city around 1824 and soon "developed depravity under the influence of whiskey."[4] When drunk, Burkhardt went looking for a fight. His favorite victims were African Americans, whose homes he often vandalized. One night in 1836, Burkhardt and the chain gang attacked the home of James Overall, a prominent African American land speculator and church trustee. But Overall refused to stand aside as his home was ransacked. As they broke down the door, "he fired his shotgun, wounding one man." The assailants fled, but Overall knew they would soon return for revenge. He sent word to attorney Calvin Fletcher, who later reported that he had assembled a constable and a considerable number of other prominent citizens to defend Overall against the outrageous mob headed by Burkhardt. They ordered Burkhardt to leave town, "immediately and permanently." One unruly chain gang member, David Leach was arrested for breach of peace for shouting death threats during the incident. Burkhardt's crew knew him affectionately as Old Dave Burkhardt, or simply as Dave or Buck. Because of his immense popularity and his residence in the White River area, they may have fondly referred to their living quarters as Buck's Town, or more simply Bucktown.[5]

Comically and ironically, the decline in the popularity and legend of Old Dave Burkhardt can be traced to an incident that occurred during a religious revival. Legend has it that a local, well-respected Methodist white minister, the Reverend James Haven, conducted a religious revival at Camp Sullivan, on the west side of town (Camp Sullivan was originally the old state fairgrounds, then a Mexican prisoner of war camp, and now present-day Military Park). Burkhardt and his crew arrived and began to cause a ruckus. In the middle of his sermon, Reverend Haven respectfully pleaded with the men to be quiet, to behave, and to respect the sanctity of the service.

Their noise and raucous activity intensified. Finally, Reverend Haven left the pulpit and walked to the outskirts of the crowd to reason with the men, but to no avail. Burkhardt, seeing the minister advance, began to sing a ribald song that insulted the reverend and the crowd. Exasperated, the reverend unbuttoned his clerical collar, removed his smock, neatly folded them, and handed them to a spectator. He then grabbed Burkhardt by the throat and thrashed him mercilessly.

The beating that Burkhardt received that day at the hands of a minister was simply disgraceful. To the amusement of his crew and the crowd, he was humiliated in public, and he never regained the respect and admiration of his men. It

Fig. 2.2 Dave Burkhardt's crew working on Highway 40. Drawing by Shonna Jennings.

was reported that this incident changed the course of Burkhardt's life forever and that "he subsequently led an upright life."[6]

As a result of their experiences with the Cumberland Road construction workers, African Americans had two alternatives. First, they could peacefully coexist with this threat to the harmony in their community and suffer the inevitable indignities or slights. Second, they might organize their community against the invasion of this unsavory element of society. They likely believed that this influx of problematic behavior would be detrimental to their community. As they struggled toward freedom, they wanted assurance that nothing would impede their path. Bethel AME was the ideal institution to spearhead this movement to protect the community and to present the image of a shining city on a hill.

TWO

—ᨆ—

THE SHAME OF INDIANAPOLIS

DURING THE 1840S, THE DEMOGRAPHIC profile of Indianapolis changed because of the influx of escaped and free slaves from the South. This drastic shift in the complexion of the city alarmed a segment of the white population that harbored anti–African American sentiment. Perhaps they believed that the influx of African Americans, who would take the most menial jobs, would threaten their economic livelihood. The racial climate in Indianapolis was identical to that in many cities of the South. African Americans arriving from the South recognized the similarity and knew that they had to prepare themselves for an onslaught of inhumane treatment by the majority. Although they may have envisioned Indianapolis as an oasis of hope and promise, events publicized in newspapers throughout the state certainly disappointed them. "What must we do to be allowed to sit at the 'table of humankind'?" many African Americans wondered.

In particular, two historic events highlighted the vitriol and hatred of African Americans in some segments of the city. Fortunately, there was also a progressive, egalitarian, nonracist segment of the majority community that took issue with this blatant racism and fought to eliminate it. These citizens undoubtedly encountered intense criticism and backlash, but they persisted. And although the African Americans were continually under attack, they continued their march toward freedom.

The first of these events occurred on Independence Day in 1845. The following story appeared in the July 16, 1845, edition of the *New York Times* in reference to a report that had appeared in the July 5 edition of the *Indianapolis Sentinel*.

John Tucker was a former slave from Kentucky who purchased his freedom and relocated to Indianapolis in the 1830s. He was a husband, a father, and a farmer who was considered by members of the community to be a "very peaceable colored man." He served as a trustee at the Bethel African-Methodist Episcopal Church and was involved in the struggle for basic civil rights for African Americans. On July 4, as Tucker was walking down Illinois Street near Michigan Avenue, he was confronted by a crowd of rowdy, white revelers celebrating the holiday. Suddenly, as he passed the crowd, he received a blow to the head administered by Nicholas Wood, who was one of the revelers. Tucker instinctively coiled his body to protect himself from other blows, and that reaction excited the crowd and its anger intensified (fig. 3.1).

Instantly, he was set upon by other members of the mob as white onlookers gazed with amusement and refused to assist him. He was beaten mercilessly with clubs, bricks, and bats. Tucker's skull was fractured by a blow "that would have felled an ox." He fell to the pavement, where he ultimately died, but not without defending himself with "desperate determination." According to the *Times*, one white assailant received a "severe cut in the side of his head from a brickbat."[1]

Reverend Henry Ward Beecher—pastor of the Second Presbyterian Church on Governor's Circle (modern-day Monument Circle), an abolitionist, and the brother of Harriet Beecher Stowe (an abolitionist and later the author of the antislavery book *Uncle Tom's Cabin*)—was holding a service that evening. Afterward, as he departed the church, he saw a crowd assembled to the north on Illinois Street. He heard high-pitched screams and hurried to the scene. As he approached the mob, they cried, "The niggers are getting too cursed thick, and ought to be thinned out! I would as lief [gladly] kill a nigger as an Ox! Damn them, I wish everyone was shot and the abolitionist too!" Tucker lay before him on the sidewalk with blood rushing from his skull. His eyes were dilated, and he was dead.

A prominent white citizen, Calvin Fletcher, the first practicing attorney in Indianapolis, a state senator, and an abolitionist, raised money to fund the prosecution of the case and bring the guilty parties to justice. But Fletcher's efforts were not completely realized. Of the three white men implicated in the murder, only one, Wood, was found guilty of manslaughter; Edward Davis was acquitted, and James Ballinger disappeared from town.[2]

As the state of Indiana attempted to gain some semblance of compassion and respectability and recover from the murder of John Tucker, the second sensational case captured newspaper headlines from coast to coast. John Freeman was born as a free Black man in Prince Edward County, Virginia, in March 1807. In 1831, he moved to Walton, Georgia, and thirteen years later he arrived in Indianapolis. He joined the Second Presbyterian Church under the pastorate

Fig. 3.1 John Tucker attacked in downtown Indianapolis on Independence Day 1845.
Drawing by Shonna Jennings.

of Henry Ward Beecher and became a sexton and later a member of the colored Second Baptist Church. Between 1844 and 1849, he married Letitia Warner and purchased property on North Meridian Street and operated an oyster restaurant on Washington Street.

On June 20, 1853, Pleasant Ellington, a Kentucky native and slave owner who resided in Preston, Platte County, Missouri, arrived in Indianapolis. He visited the home of James and Lorenzo Githens, and while there, he met Freeman, who was a guest of the house.

Instantly, Ellington was convinced that Freeman was his former slave who had escaped servitude in Missouri, and he cleverly took measures to recover his property. Ellington devised a scheme to trick Freeman into going to the Marion County Circuit Court, where charges could be filed against him. The Githens brothers had introduced Ellington to US Deputy Marshal J. H. Stopp, who informed Freeman that the US commissioner and former mayor William Sullivan wished to speak to him. When Freeman entered the circuit court, he met Ellington and Stopp (fig. 3.2).

Immediately, Ellington accused Freeman of being a runaway slave named Sam, whom he had owned in Missouri and of whom he had been in hot pursuit for seventeen years. Allegedly, he had proof that Freeman was his property, and to substantiate his claim, he offered knowledge of identifiable characteristics of Sam's body. Ellington claimed that Sam had a burn mark on his left leg, scars on his back, and "peculiarly small ears and large feet."[3] Freeman was thrown in jail, where he remained for sixty days. His wife went to the Marion County Circuit Court and to prove his freedom presented free papers signed by the most prominent slave owners in the South.

The court informed Mrs. Freeman that these papers did not supersede the federal Fugitive Slave Law of 1850, and her husband remained in jail to be sent to Kentucky later that day. Distraught, and with her child in her arms, she wandered through the streets informing anyone who would listen of her husband's painful and unjust ordeal. By chance, she encountered a stranger who listened carefully to her plea and then to her surprise announced, "Madame, my name is John Coburn. I am an abolitionist and a lawyer. The fugitive slave law is a hard one to combat, but I will see that your husband is not (taken) out of town until he has had his trial. I will get our papers at once to stop the proceedings in the case."[4] As a precautionary measure, Mrs. Freeman hired a guard and paid him two dollars daily to ensure that her husband would not be spirited at night to Missouri and sent into slavery.

Newspaper accounts that covered this sensational story throughout the country prompted sympathetic readers to volunteer information that might solve the case and free John Freeman. Information received indicated that the

Fig. 3.2 John Freeman in court fighting for his freedom. Drawing by Shonna Jennings.

suspected former slave may have been living in Canada under an alias. Coburn and his law partner Lucien Barbour traveled to Canada, and for many days, they searched Montreal for a person who matched the physical characteristics described by Ellington. Finally, they located Sam, who had lived with the alias McConnell. Sam accommodated Coburn by showing him the burn mark on his left leg and scars on his back, and Coburn and Barbour plainly observed his peculiarly small ears and unbelievably big feet. Immediately, both attorneys returned to Indianapolis and presented the evidence to the court, whereupon Freeman was freed from jail. Freeman sued both Ellington and Stopp for $1,300, and the court allowed him to collect $2,000. Ellington scoffed at the decision and fled to Saint Louis, and Freeman did not receive a penny.

Freeman remained in Indianapolis, but after Union forces were defeated at the Battle of Bull Run of July 21, 1861, fought near Prince William County, Virginia, he questioned the vitality of those forces. In the fall of 1863 or spring of 1864, Freeman and his wife, Letitia, moved to Canada, where they had a daughter, Hattie, four years later. In 1870, the family moved to Topeka, Kansas, and they remained there until their deaths. John Freeman died October 5, 1902, and Letitia Warner Freeman died April 10, 1910.[5]

—〰—

FOUR

LIFE, LIBERTY, AND THE PURSUIT OF HAPPINESS

PRIOR TO THE CIVIL WAR, African Americans fled the South in great numbers, chased by agents of slave owners with snarling dogs nipping at their heels. These agents were determined to capture the slaves and return them to their slave masters and a life of servitude for a handsome bounty. Assuredly, fugitive slaves assumed that their community was the sole commodity sought by this industry and did not realize that this dragnet of intrigue caught individuals of the majority community as well. They were surprised to discover that, in some instances, members of the majority community were mistaken for African Americans and taken into custody in an attempt to deliver them to slave masters. Also, they may have been surprised to learn that, in some instances, members of their own community collaborated with slave owners for monetary gains. Caught up in this dilemma, African Americans may have considered themselves to be caught between the proverbial rock and a hard place. Nevertheless, African Americans in Indiana and other states continued to strive toward freedom.[1]

During this period, African Americans from other cities in Indiana migrated to Indianapolis for better educational and employment opportunities and brought stories documenting their plight. They related horrific events to Blacks in Indianapolis to make them more cognizant of the severity of societal problems throughout Indiana. There were many biracial or pejoratively classified mulattoes who were racially indistinguishable. Some passed for white to receive better treatment. Others did not and were concerned about the well-being of their relatives in their former residences. Both groups heard stories of slave catchers that traveled to the North to capture free persons of color or escaped slaves to return to the South for monetary gains. They feared their relatives' apprehension and transport into the clutches of slavery. One story about such an event shocked African Americans in Indianapolis.

The *Underground Railroad in Floyd County, Indiana* by Pamela R. Peters recounts the story of an African American family that collaborated with southern slave catchers to apprehend fugitive slaves and free Blacks. She writes that "an African-American family in the Knobs took the fugitives in and kept them for two days. The runaway slaves, thinking that the family was protecting them and attempting to send them farther north, trusted them explicitly. However, the family betrayed the fugitives, probably to collect a reward, and notified authorities in Louisville [Kentucky]."[2] In this instance, racism, injustice, and deception were polychromatic.

The period between 1850 and 1860 must have perplexed African Americans arriving in Indianapolis. On one hand, they were being warmly welcomed by the members of Bethel AME Church, who wanted to make their transition to city life as fluid and comfortable as possible. On the other hand, they sensed that their presence was not appreciated and was under intense scrutiny.

Legal machinery had already been set in motion to regulate the movement of the recently arrived African Americans. Fugitive slave laws protected the property rights of slave owners in the southern states. Many of the politicians who favored these laws were, in fact, slave owners themselves and wanted to craft legislation to protect their interests. Fearing economic loss, they designed laws with harsh penalties for escaped slaves and all parties who aided their escape.[3]

During this time, a new industry developed with an economic incentive to capture and return escaped slaves to servitude. Slave catchers were generally lower-class, impoverished, landless southern whites—known in common parlance as "poor white trash"—who capitalized on the institution of slavery. They made intense efforts to capture the escaped slaves and return them to their "rightful owners" for a specified amount of money. Searching the back roads, thickets, and tall brush, slave catchers were known to travel to northern cities where slavery was illegal, capture escaped slaves, and return them to their masters in southern states. In many cases the Quaker community battled the slave catchers in the court of law to block the return of escaped slaves. The issue of slavery was hotly debated in the halls of Congress in Washington, on the floor of the state legislature in Indianapolis, and elsewhere. It was the monumental issue that led the United States into the most important controversy of the century: the Civil War. In the middle of the nineteenth century, many slave owners contracted slave catchers to enter Indiana, apprehend escaped slaves, and return them to the South. But one monumental case from November 1850 illustrated the draconian and inhumane dimensions of the Fugitive Slave Act of 1850 and captured the attention of the nation.

According to Pamela Peters in *The Underground Railroad in Floyd County, Indiana*, "Dennis Framell of Arkansas traveled to New Albany to recover three individuals; a woman, her daughter and grandson who he believed were his property." The case attracted heightened public interest because the defendants appeared to be white and devoid of African ancestry. The boy attended school with white children, "mingling with white children, no one suspecting him of being aught else than white like ourselves," and the woman claimed that her husband had been killed by Indians and she and her daughter captured. Further, she declared that they had lived with the Indians in Arkansas and "had never been treated as slaves."[4]

Initially, the case was argued before Judge Jared C. Jocelyn and appealed by writ of habeas corpus to Judge Huntington of the US Court of Appeals. The court determined that a delay allowing evidence from the defendants' former residence to arrive would postpone the trial indefinitely. The most outstanding attorneys of the city volunteered their services to defend the three individuals. On November 29, 1850, a US marshal for the District of Southern Indiana appeared in court with orders to return the defendants to Framell because Arkansas had provided no evidence to substantiate their identities. Immediately, they were transferred to Louisville, Kentucky, and imprisoned in a slave pen.

The case received national coverage from newspapers in Washington, DC, New York, Philadelphia, and other eastern cities. The citizens of New Albany and Louisville raised $600 demanded by Framell. The case was settled, and the three defendants were released and returned to New Albany. The national coverage of this case turned many Indiana citizens against the Fugitive Slave Law because it illustrated the fact that defendants were refused the right to testify in their own defense.[5]

The resolution of this case proved to be an omen for the social, political, legal, and economic climate that faced people of color who might enter the state. Given that no "welcome mat" was laid before them as they traveled to Indianapolis from many points south, the following questions arise: Who were these early African Americans who had fled the South in their quest for freedom? What churches did they attend? What obstacles did they have to overcome in their transition from a culture of slavery to freedom? These and other seemingly mundane questions must be addressed if one is to understand the social, economic, political, and religious atmosphere of Indianapolis during the middle of the nineteenth century.

The animus generated among certain segments of the majority population in reference to newly arrived Blacks increased, and measures were contemplated to combat what they saw as a "Negro invasion." Legal machinations revved up. In 1850, delegates from throughout the state traveled to Indianapolis to craft a new state constitution. The most pressing political issue in that judicial discourse was the exclusion of Blacks from the state of Indiana. As a consequence, a decidedly "anti-Negro" sentiment filled the chambers. The delegates proposed that the state had been overrun by Blacks, and to remedy this problem, they adopted article 13 of the Indiana State Constitution. It banned Negro migration into the state and promoted colonization. It declared, "No Negro or mulatto shall come into or settle in the State, after adoption of this Constitution."[6] This sentiment of anti-Negro exclusion was not new. It hearkened back to the days of the birth of the nation when George Washington's nephew Thomas Bushrod led a campaign to encourage states to organize colonization societies and appropriate money to establish a colony in Africa where Negro slaves could be sent. In 1821, Liberia, located on the west coast of Africa, was founded, and its capital, Monrovia, was named in honor of President James Monroe.

"NEGROES, YAW GO BACK TO AFRICA!"

FROM THE EARLY DAYS OF Indianapolis in the 1820s, with a few African Americans who were maids and male servants to prominent families, to the middle of the nineteenth century, the population of African Americans in Indiana in general and Indianapolis in specific ballooned considerably. Historian Emma Lou Thornbrough reports that in 1860 the Census listed 498 African Americans, which constituted a mere 2.6 percent of the total population. This demographic changed considerably during the following decades.[1] On many occasions in the late-evening or early-morning hours, groups of escaped African American slaves clandestinely arrived, were spirited to downtown, and rapped on the doors of the Bethel African-Methodist Episcopal (AME) Church in search of food, lodging, and clothing. Slowly, the majority community noticed this rapid increase of African Americans in the city and became increasingly alarmed and determined to initiate measures to combat it.

The alarm bells rang loudly, resonating from Indianapolis to Washington, DC. From the floor of the state government in Indiana to the halls of Congress, legislators were contacted and pressured by their constituents to address the problem of the influx of African Americans in their communities. In Indianapolis, legislators dealt with questions related to the drastic change in city demographics: What can we do to stem the tide of these Negroes? Will they become a burden on our city government? What can we do to run them out of town? Will crime in our dear city increase? Legislators reacted accordingly.

Statesmen in Washington had already crafted legal machinations to address the problem. One of the most egregious strategies employed in Indianapolis as a directive of federal and state legislation was to identify prominent African American leaders as coconspirators. These leaders, some of whom were ministers, were encouraged to convince the African American community that the solution to the problem of racism in Indianapolis was to return to Africa.

The conspirators did not care that the overwhelming majority of the African Americans in Indianapolis were born in America to families that had resided in the country for several generations. Their only concern was to rid Indianapolis of the perceived onslaught of undesirables. African Americans in Indianapolis, determined to be bona fide, free citizens, joined forces to thwart this malicious plan. Anti–African American sentiment was not only a topic of discussion in general social intercourse but also a cause of concern in other institutions.

Luman Jones was a member of the Seventy-Ninth Indiana Regiment Company E., and although engaged in a heated battle with Confederate forces, he subscribed to elements of racism espoused by Confederate soldiers. In a letter written to his wife, Elizabeth, he revealed his hatred toward African Americans: "I long to see the day when there will not be a Nigger in the United States. I want them all sent away to a country by themselves and let the Whites be by themselves, to work out there [sic] salvation the best they can."

Although the South was reputed to be the most conservative and racist region of America because of its history of slavery and oppression of persons of color, including Native Americans and African Americans, other regions of America were reputed to be little better. Indiana was geographically located in the North, above the Mason Dixon Line (a line, surveyed by Charles Mason and Jeremiah Dixon between 1763 and 1767, that became the border between the northern United States and the southern United States), but many of its inhabitants shared southern sentiment and harbored feelings of hatred, animosity, and racism toward African Americans. Poor whites who depended on agricultural and other forms of menial employment feared the threat of competition in the labor force. Some white Americans longed for the day of African American repatriation to Africa.

To understand and appreciate the genesis of this "anti–African American/ back-to-Africa" movement, one must turn to the early 1800s and observe the Indiana state legislators in action. One could definitely make a philosophical connection between their concerns and the development of this movement in Indianapolis five decades later. The seeds were planted in these august halls of justice, and the flower of racial hatred and disenfranchisement bloomed later.

In the Indiana General Assembly in 1816, Robert Price articulated the general feeling succinctly in his statement of protest and concern: "We don't want them up north. . . . Let the curse stay in the south."[2] Assembly members in Indianapolis were deeply concerned with the colonization movement, a campaign to repatriate African Americans to Liberia. As more African Americans, including both free and escaped slaves, fled the South, this topic demanded considerable attention among the general public. The question of colonization as a solution to the "Negro problem" was hotly debated in homes, churches, assembly halls, and other public forums throughout the state of Indiana. As early as the founding of the United States, President Thomas Jefferson and other prominent political leaders of the Revolutionary era proposed colonization as a solution to the paradox of freedom and liberty in America. These leaders championed the preamble to the Declaration of Independence, which reads, "We hold these truths to be self-evident that all men are created equal . . . endowed by their Creator with certain unalienable Rights, that among these are life, liberty and the pursuit of happiness," but at the same time, they justified the enslavement of African Americans. Their philosophy was impregnated with the rationale that African Americans were subhuman and not worthy of American citizenship. Thomas Bushrod, George Washington's nephew, urged states to organize colonization societies to raise money to establish settlements on the African coast where African Americans could be sent. He expressed the contradictory logic of his uncle and other revolutionary leaders of the era.[3]

In 1817, Samuel Milroy, a member of the Indiana General Assembly, introduced a resolution to colonize Blacks in the far west, preferably in the state of Oregon. Two years later, President James Monroe signed an act of Congress that included the stipulation "to send beyond the limits of the United States all captured Negroes and to appoint agents, residing on the coast of Africa, to receive them."[4]

On January 20, 1820, members of the Indiana General Assembly met in Corydon, Indiana, and formed the American Colonization Society. Their primary goal was to rid Indiana of African Americans and return them to their native soil in Africa. After much discussion, they agreed that "the principle and practice of slavery, are wholly unrecognized with the constitution of the American government and the best feelings of the American government and the feelings of human nature . . . no exertions which can properly be made for the eradication of this great evil, should be withheld; and that the use of every means which can justly be resorted to, be recommended to the citizens of this State, to check its extension and to accomplish its abolition as far as practicable."[5]

On February 7, 1825, the Indiana General Assembly met in Indianapolis and approved a joint resolution that provided for the gradual emancipation of slaves and foreign colonization. Governor James Brown Ray, in his 1829 address to the assembly, strongly supported the goals of the colonization movement. He opined that the expatriation of Blacks to Africa would be the greatest accomplishment of the age: "We long to celebrate the jubilee of freedom—of general and unconditional emancipation, of every soul held in bondage, because his skin is dark. We look forward with fervent hope, to the important era, when we shall see them wending their way across the Atlantic" so that "the next generation might be saved the mortifying spectacle, of beholding the manacled African suffering in his fetters, in the temple of human freedom."[6]

In spite of the overwhelming support for the idea of colonialization in Indiana, there were dissenting voices that questioned the motives of this movement. Benjamin Lundy, an American Quaker from New Jersey who established several antislavery newspapers, initially adopted the tenets of this movement but later had reservations. He stated, "I am not anxious to support this measure any further than it will serve the cause of emancipation." He predicted that it would not be possible to colonize every Black in the United States "or that it will be necessary that they should be." Lundy believed that colonization should only pave "the way for the completion of that grand and benevolent work, the Abolition of Slavery." Quakers argued that colonization, founded on principles that unfairly forced the expatriation of Africans "as a condition to the slaves being set at liberty, is unjust and oppressive."[7]

Some proponents of this movement, including members of the Indiana General Assembly, may have found some of its tenets problematic or contradictory. On one hand, many benevolent, white Christians recognized the evil of America's slavery and wished to abolish the system because they deemed it antithetical to the scriptures of the Bible. On the other hand, some recognized the competition African Americans presented to poor whites in the procurement of agricultural employment and general menial labor. Some rationalized that this economic competition might prove detrimental to the economy and that the repatriation of African Americans to Africa would solve the problem. They believed that Blacks would be happier in a more equitable and harmonious environment wherein their skin color would not determine their treatment and acceptance in society.

The Reverend Benjamin Taylor Kavanaugh, of Louisville, Kentucky, was a proponent of the colonization movement (fig. 5.1). During one of his speeches to the American Colonization Society, in reference to the motives of the anti-colonization and abolitionist movements, he stated: "They seemed disposed to spare no labor or pains, in searching for all the evils in our disordered world. . . . But where is the remedy? The abolitionists aim at arriving the slave and his master over the head of the FEDERAL CONSTITUTION, which is, in its very nature, highly seditious, if not treasonable."[8]

Kavanaugh's concern for the plight of the emancipated slave was highly questionable. Although he was a minister in the Methodist Episcopal Church and

Fig. 5.1 Benjamin T. Kavanaugh, early colonization proponent.
Drawing by Shonna Jennings.

preached the love and compassion of his fellow humans in the biblical scriptures from the Sunday pulpit, he later became chaplain and missionary of the Confederate Army, during the Civil War. He worked under the command of Major General Sterling "Old Pap" Price, best known for his defeat in the Battles of Pea Ridge (Battle of Elkhorn Tavern) and Westport during the Civil War. His benevolent motives most likely cloaked his disdain for African Americans and his desire to rid Indianapolis of more economically advantaged African Americans. Once he removed them, he would be able to concentrate on destabilizing and victimizing the less fortunate Black populace. The Methodist Episcopal Church, which originally was anti-elitist and antislavery, debated the issue of slavery at its conferences. Churches in the North viewed slavery as an abomination of the teachings of Jesus Christ and violently opposed the institution, while its congregants in the South regarded slavery as one of the building blocks of their economy. In 1844, at a general conference convened in New York, the church split into two factions, with the northern churches objecting to slavery and the southern churches accepting it. Kavanaugh's beliefs compelled him to join the southern faction.[9]

In 1850, the Indiana General Assembly met in Corydon, Indiana, to formulate a new state constitution, and the fervor previously generated by the American Colonization Society was reinvigorated. One of the first questions addressed concerned the "Negro problem" in Indiana. Many delegates felt that Indiana had been inundated with Blacks and that measures should be taken to reverse this course. Article 13 of the Indiana State Constitution was introduced, forbidding the entry of Negroes into the state and establishing a colonization movement to return the Negroes to Africa, even though many of them either were born in America or had family who had resided there for several generations. The article stipulated that "no Negro or mulatto shall come into or settle in the state." It was presented to the public in a referendum, and 80 percent voted to approve the article.[10]

In effect, this law subjected every free Black in Indiana to apprehension by a slave catcher. The slave catcher merely went to court and swore to the justice of the peace that their captive was a fugitive slave. The slave catcher then had the right to return the captive to servitude in the South and receive a handsome bounty for his apprehension services. The slave did not have a legal recourse in this matter.[11]

The Indianapolis Bethel African-Methodist Episcopal (AME) Church served as the headquarters where many citizens, regardless of race, met to discuss issues that affected the African America community. Many enlightened citizens saw the colonization movement as a clandestine attempt to eliminate the class of more prosperous and educated African Americans who fought for the freedom and welfare of their less fortunate siblings. Ironically, some Black and white advocates of the colonization movement thought that the presence of African American colonists in Africa would disrupt the slave trade and help Christianize and civilize indigenous ethnic groups. In many of the forums, these devious schemes were extensively discussed.[12]

As a result of the African American community's cautious and skeptical response to this movement, the colonizationists devised a new "pied piper effect" (a strategy in which a charismatic leader made irresponsible promises to attract gullible followers) to circumvent suspicion. They selected Reverend Willis Revels, pastor of Bethel AME Church, who enjoyed unquestionable loyalty from his congregation and fellow African Americans. They reasoned that he could assuage the ill feelings of skeptics and convince them that repatriation to Liberia would solve their social, political, and economic problems. Many forum participants were outraged by the suggestion that they should leave Indianapolis and travel to a distant destination about which they were devoid of knowledge and history. Ultimately, in the wake of receiving numerous angry letters and hot words delivered in the forums, Revels relented, resigned his post, and reversed his course of action.[13]

Undaunted by African Americans' negative reaction to the colonization movement and their scathing rebuke of Revels, the colonizationists formulated a scheme to convince skeptics with an advertisement campaign. In June 1853, the Reverend James Mitchell, a young Methodist minister from Franklin, Indiana, who had replaced Kavanaugh as agent of the Indiana Colonization Society, distributed colonization subscriptions to county treasurers to finance a settlement in Liberia for free African Americans. He longed to bring Blacks to Liberia so that they could survey the country and return to America with favorable accounts that would entice more Blacks to migrate. With that in mind, he obtained the services of a Black AME minister from Madison, Indiana, John McKay.

In April 1853, McKay and six emigrants departed from Norfolk, Virginia, on the ship *Banshee* for the thirty-four-day expedition to Cape Mount, Liberia. Upon arrival, they met a Hoosier named William W. Findlay, from Covington, Indiana, who emigrated in March 1850 aboard the ship *D. C. Foster* with his wife, Frances, and six children. Upon McKay's return to the United States, fourteen more Black Hoosiers applied to emigrate to Liberia, and in November 1853, McKay escorted them from Baltimore, Maryland. The same year, he intended to escort fifty more Black Hoosiers, but they changed their minds because of pressure exerted upon them by Black anticolonizationists from Indiana.[14]

Fig. 5.2 Passenger ship to Liberia. Drawing by Shonna Jennings.

From February 1840 until November 1862, the year after the outbreak of the Civil War, more than eighty African Americans immigrated to Liberia from Indiana (fig. 5.2). The ships' passenger list named the small towns of Covington, Madison, Jackson County, Lafayette, Attica, Vincennes, Princeton, Wayne County, Euphrasia, and Montezuma (fig. 5.3). During these years of travel, ship records included information about the passengers who successfully completed the voyage. Unfortunately, the records indicated that not all survived; the deceased included three adults (Henry Frye, Salina Clay, and Martha Clay) and five children (F. D. Frye, one year old; infant Frye, two days old; Clay Tompkins, three years old; Isabella Ladd, four months old; and Charlotte Simms, six years old). Cornelius Simms, a contemporary of Mary Bateman-Clark (who fought for and won her freedom in a sensational case that involved slavery and indentured

Indiana Emigrants to Liberia

Name (age)	Home	Ship	Name (age)	Home	Ship
February 1840			Cornelius Simms (49)	Vincennes	
Names not available		Saluda	Elizabeth (33)		
(5 emigrants)			Charles (18)		
March 1850			William (14)		
William W. Findlay (36)	Covington	D. C. Foster	Sarah (12)		
Frances (27)			George W. (10)		
Sarah J. (11)			Charlotte (6) - died whooping cough		
Samuel (9)			Thomas J. (4)		
W. W. (8)			Jacob Stephenson (56)	Princeton	
H. J. (6)			Harrison (14)		
C. S. (3)			Robert (12)		
J. (1)			Charles (10)		
Henry Fry (48) - died	Covington		James W. (8)		
Sarah (27)			David Matthews (37)	Wayne County	
Isabella (11)			Alley (28)		
Elizabeth (7)			William H. (12)		
H. (5)			Frederick (7)		
Eliza (9)			David (2)		
C. (3)			Rev. John McKay (39)	Madison	(escort for party)
F. D. (1) - died			Samuel Coleman	Attica - source: ACS records - List of emigrants	
Infant (2 days) - died					
February 1851			**November 1854**		
Peter Tompkins (44)	Madison	Brig Alida	Lamar (Tamar?) Peters (50)		Euphrasia
- died January 1852			George (30)		
Harriet (45)			Alexander (25)		
Salina Clay (21) - died			Priscilla (20)		
Martha Clay (18) - died			Mary (18)		
Ann Eliza Clay (17)			Simon (6)		
Emily Jane Clay (15) - died January 9, 1851			Charles (4)		
Josiah Tompkins (7)			Mary (2)		
Clay Tompkins (3) - died August 5, 1851			Martha (20)		
November 1852			Rachel (23)		
Samuel B. Webster (90)	Lafayette	Barque Shirley	William Robinson (50)		
April 1853			Mary (30)		
Elvin Ash (44)	Jackson Co.	Banshee	Emily (17)		
Lucinda (45)			Mary (16)		
Josephine (10)			John D. Stewart (20)		
Gabriel (8)			The above emigrants may be from Putnam County and Montezuma, Indiana.		
Nice (4)			**November 1859**		
Nancy J. (2)			Rev. M. M. Clark		M. C. Stevens
November 1853			There should be two more emigrants on this ship from Indiana.		
Joseph Ladd (28)	Attica	Banshee	**November 1862**		
Susan (17)			Isabella Harris (30)		M. C. Stevens
George W. (2 mos.)			J. H. Harris (34)		
William Brown (45)					
Susan (28)					
John (4)					
Isabella (4 mos.) - died whooping cough					

Sources: African Repository and Colonial Journal; Tom W. Shick, "Emigrants to Liberia, 1820-1843," Liberian Studies Research Working Paper No. 2 (Newark, Del., 1971); Robert T. Brown, "Immigrants to Liberia, 1848 to 1865," Liberian Studies Research Working Paper No. 7 (Philadelphia, 1980).

Fig. 5.3 List of passengers on ship to Liberia. Courtesy of the Indiana Historical Bureau, a division of the Indiana State Library.

servitude in Vincennes, Indiana, in the early nineteenth century), along with his family, boarded the ship *Saluda* and sailed to Liberia in 1840.[15]

Interestingly, in the middle of the nineteenth century, while slaves were being captured and transported to America, there were international attempts to terminate the industry. In 1842, both the United States and Great Britain signed the Webster-Ashburton Treaty, which deemed illegal the transport of captured Africans from the coast of Africa. Both countries dispatched their naval vessels to the west coast of Africa, referred to in some literature as the "Barbary Coast," to intercept ships transporting slaves captured in Africa. These ships were called squadrons, and one of the earliest American squadron ships patrolled the west coast of Africa, but because the secretary of the navy, Abel Parker Upshur, was a southerner and an extreme supporter of slavery and states' rights, he assigned few ships to patrol the coast.[16]

—ɯ—

THE CIVIL WAR YEARS AND BEYOND

DURING THE MIDDLE OF THE nineteenth century, as the influx of African Americans increased in Indianapolis, some migrants from the South evaluated their degree of freedom and quality of life in the North as opposed to the horrific circumstances they had faced in the South. Many were pleased with the acquisition of more basic rights and wanted to ingratiate themselves and be accepted as equals by the majority community. They wanted to demonstrate that they were worthy of their new station in life and were willing to live in harmony with other residents in the city. However, many voices from the majority community called for caution in the consideration of "Negro migration" and its consequences. A letter to the *Indianapolis Sentinel* in April 1862 reported that Indianapolis and the towns along the Ohio River were rapidly "filling up with strange Africans." These opposing sentiments from migrants and established residents were destined to collide.

Then came the outbreak of the Civil War. Could this war give African Americans the opportunity to test their mettle and prove their loyalty? African Americans in Indianapolis maintained their patriotism despite many public displays of disrespect and contempt. The sentiment appears in this declaration from a Negro student in 1864: "The war is now in part *our war*, and the free colored men of the North must help fight it."[1] The more thoughtful African Americans of Indiana recognized the challenge that the conflict between the states presented to their population. Samuel G. Smothers of the Union Literary Institute wrote:

> The time has now come for intelligent, decisive and energetic action on our part. For thirty years, we have been lecturing, talking and praying for the liberation of our enslaved brethren. God has answered our prayers, and our brethren are being liberated by the thousands. The wonderful changes

which are now taking place in our condition, brings upon us new duties. The first and most important of these duties is to stand by and defend the government. Our liberties, our interests and our happiness, in common with other citizens, depends upon the fate of this government. If the government stands, our liberties are secure; if the government falls, we will be doomed to life-long bondage of chains. It is true that we do not enjoy in some of the States all the rights and privileges of other citizens enjoy, but our condition is certainly far better than it would be under Jeff. Davis' [Jefferson Davis, President of the Confederacy] rule. Again, to fight in defense of the government, will confer lasting honor upon us and our posterity, and secure for us the respect and admiration of our white fellow-citizens.

Smothers believed that education was the key to gaining acceptance among some segments of the majority community and that an excellent African American educational institution was essential for upward mobility.[2] The Union Literary Institute was an invaluable component of African American liberation. Predating the Civil War, this school, established in Randolph County to educate freed slaves, provided "the most significant and successful experiment in Negro education."[3] Its constitution declared that the institution was principally for the "benefit of that class of the population whom the laws of Indiana at present preclude from all participation in the benefits of our public school system and further for the purpose of placing the blessings of an education in the higher branches of science within the reach of all who have not the means and facilities for the acquisition of scientific knowledge, which are always at the command of the wealthy." Unfortunately, because of the rigors imposed on it by the pending Civil War, the school closed temporarily, and in September 1864, Smothers volunteered for service in the Union Army. He declared, "I feel that the time has come when the cause of our distracted and bleeding country, and the interests of my race, require me to act rather than to talk or write.[4]

At the outbreak of the Civil War, the enforcement of article 13 of the Indiana State Constitution was relaxed as an increasing number of fugitive slaves moved into the state. Many of the fleeing slaves were from Kentucky, Tennessee, Georgia, and Mississippi. Governor Oliver P. Morton, anxious to call up a substantial number of native sons for the war and exceed his quota, looked carefully at the arriving Black slaves. On December 3, 1863, six companies of colored soldiers totaling 518 enlisted men were assembled in Indianapolis with William P. Fishback as commandant. The battalion was increased to a full regiment in Maryland and was known as the Twenty-Eighth US Colored Battalion.[5] This occurred shortly after President Abraham Lincoln signed the Emancipation Proclamation on January 1, 1863. The soldiers of this battalion demonstrated their true grit at the Battle of the Crater, in which half of their soldiers were either killed or wounded.[6] This sacrifice proved them to be true, patriotic Americans worthy of citizenship.

The news of African American troops enlisted to fight in the war was not well received by some white officers and enlisted men. They saw Blacks as inherently inferior and believed that African Americans did not have the mental, moral, or physical capacity to adequately perform their duties. Further, they felt that the lives of many white soldiers would be in jeopardy if Blacks were allowed to carry arms and to fight on the battlefields.[7]

A number of white officers questioned their commissions and threatened to resign in response to President Lincoln's signing of the Emancipation Proclamation. They believed that the Civil War was an unjust war that would ultimately elevate Blacks to a higher station in society and threaten the philosophy of white supremacy to which some soldiers subscribed. Some white soldiers believed that if the Union Army triumphed and consequently instituted a policy of emancipation, a multitude of Blacks would overpopulate cities in the North. Their numbers would be so great that law and order could not control them. Stephen Miller, a wounded soldier from Indiana who was recuperating in a Louisville, Kentucky, military hospital, wrote a vitriolic letter to his parents in which he expressed his outrage concerning the passage of the Emancipation Proclamation: "As soon as I get my money I am coming home I don't care if the(y) call it deserting or not. . . . I did not volunter [sic] to fight to free the niggers and I guess that(s) what that old black Abolition Abe is at now. . . . If he dont go at trying to free niggers I will come back in to the service again but if he goes at that I shall never shoulder a gun again to fight the rebels."[8] Although Indiana was considered a northern state, located above the Mason-Dixon Line, because of its close proximity to Kentucky and Tennessee, there was a considerable amount of support for the South's secession from the Union.

Many of the detractors who subscribed to such racist beliefs of Black inferiority protected the institutions of southern heritage of which they were products. Southern heritage, in the form of norms, mores, and folkways, was often transported from southern states to Indianapolis with the arrival of white citizens. After the conclusion of the Civil War, until the turn of the twentieth century, African Americans left southern states, mainly Kentucky, Tennessee, Arkansas, and Mississippi, and relocated to Indianapolis. Article 13 of the 1851 Indiana State Constitution was superseded by federal legislation and court decisions, including the Thirteenth Amendment, which stipulated that slavery and involuntary servitude would be abolished; the Fourteenth Amendment, which stipulated that the rights of all citizens would be equally protected under the law; and the 1866 Civil Rights Act, which stipulated that all persons born in the United States were citizens without regard to race, color, or previous conditions.

SEVEN

POST–CIVIL WAR ACHIEVEMENT

THE PERIOD AFTER THE CIVIL WAR compelled African Americans to be more introspective in the search for equality. They recognized that Black Union soldiers fought alongside their white counterparts and shed blood on the soil of Virginia in the Battle of the Crater. Should this great feat and sacrifice not prove their loyalty? What measures should they take to assure the majority community that they were law-abiding, patriotic Americans worthy of citizenship? Some more progressive and better-educated African Americans may have presumed that education, industry, and commerce would help them gain the respect of the majority citizenry. In many instances, to ingratiate themselves with the majority, upwardly mobile African American men imitated the majority family unit. They married lighter-complexioned African American women who fit the ideal of European beauty. They made sure that their spouses were identifiably African American and not Caucasian for fear of violating a societal taboo: interracial marriage. These strategies were of the utmost importance to enterprising African Americans during this period, according to historian Eunice Brewer-Trotter.[1]

There were African American businesses in Indianapolis in the 1860s, many of which were small enterprises not listed in the *Indianapolis City Directory*. Many were small "Mom and Pop" storefronts that operated on minimal capital, according to Paul Mullins, director of the department of anthropology at Indiana University–Purdue University at Indianapolis. On Indiana Avenue, there were enterprising African Americans who recognized the importance of commerce and joined the business class. They were admired by members of the African American community for their quality of industry, determination, and business acumen.

Fig. 7.1 Nancy Smothers, the first African American business owner on Indiana Avenue. She fed Union soldiers during the Civil War. Courtesy of Thomas Ridley.

Fig. 7.2 Smothers's grocery store, circa 1860. Drawing by Shonna Jennings.

Among those joining the business class was Nancy Smothers (fig. 7.1), wife of Samuel Smothers, aforementioned as an educator in the Union Literary Institute. Nancy, a native of the Carolinas, was previously married and was the widow of a black slave, Thomas Bushrod who was named after his white slave owner. It was reportedly common knowledge in the slave community that the slave owner, Thomas Bushrod, was the nephew of President George Washington and later a proponent of the American Colonization Movement.[2]

During the following decades heading to the turn of the nineteenth century, the Smotherses expanded their commercial enterprises to include a boarding house, restaurant (fig. 7.2), clothing store, and beanery. During the Civil War, Nancy Smothers fed Union soldiers stationed at Military Park for a nickel a meal, and she was one of the founders of Bethel AME Church. Her daughter, Hortense, who as an infant migrated with her family to Indianapolis in a covered wagon, later married Archibald Bowman and opened the first African American theater at 513 Indiana Avenue in the early twentieth century.

The institution of education was very important to upwardly mobile African Americans in Indianapolis during the mid-nineteenth century, and several individuals made outstanding contributions to it. For socially prominent African Americans, education was a vehicle for the social, economic, and political advancement that would bring about freedom, respect, and acceptance.

African American educators, in addition to the ministers and community leaders, were regarded as champions of Black progress during a time of great strife and constant struggle. Many enterprising and upwardly mobile citizens welcomed their contributions to the community and held them in high esteem. Black families encouraged their children to obtain an education in order to achieve success and improve their prospects of better social and economic possibilities in life. One influential advocate was William David McCoy (fig. 7.3), born on November 14, 1853, in Cambridge City, Indiana. He moved to Boston, Massachusetts, where he received his education in the public school system. In 1874, he relocated to Helena, Arkansas, where he served as the county superintendent of public schools and jointly owned and operated the Butler & McCoy grocery store. The grocery burned to the ground on two occasions, and many believed the fires to be the work of racist, hostile community members who were jealous of the business's success. McCoy met Celeste H. Walker, a native of Cincinnati, and married her in 1879.

That same year, he traveled to Indianapolis, where he taught at the Indianapolis Public School 24. He transferred to the Charles Sumner School 23 as principal in 1883, then returned to Public School 24 as principal in 1884. Public School 24 was later named in his honor.

In 1892, President Benjamin Harrison, the twenty-third president of the United States, appointed McCoy as minister and consul general in Liberia, a country in West Africa founded in 1821. It was established, colonized, and controlled by citizens of the United States and ex-Caribbean slaves as a colony for former African American slaves and their free Black descendants. McCoy recognized the danger of his assignment and knew that three previous ministers had died of the "African fever" on post since 1882, the last being Minister Archie Clark of Iowa. Upon his embarkation to his new assignment, his parting words seemed prophetic: "Whichever way it goes, whether I escape the fever or die, I make the majority."[3] Only a few months after arriving in Liberia, he contracted the fever, and he died on May 14, 1893, in Monrovia, Liberia. His remains were returned to Indianapolis, prepared by the Flanner and Buchanan Funeral Home, and interred in the Crown Hill Cemetery.

The great example set by William David McCoy encouraged other members of the Black community to appreciate education's value as a vehicle for upward social mobility. Whatever roadblocks stood in the way had to be removed for the community to succeed. One socially mobile African American educator

Fig. 7.3 William David McCoy, minister to Liberia, educator. Drawing by Shonna Jennings.

Fig. 7.4 Teachers assembled in front of William D. McCoy School 24.

set a standard of excellence that would be emulated by future educators in the Indianapolis Public School System.

The state crafted legislation for segregated education in 1869 and eight years later amended the law to give school districts the choice of integration or segregation. The state Civil Rights Law of 1885 prohibited racial discrimination in places of public accommodation, but this was a moot point because many public establishments such as restaurants, hotels, and department stores still did not permit Blacks to patronize their businesses.[4]

In the early 1900s, the Charles Sumner School 23 and the William D. McCoy School 24 had an impressive group of teachers who educated children on the west side of Indianapolis near the White River and Indiana Avenue (fig. 7.4). One of the most impressive, highly credentialed teachers was Gertrude Amelia Mahorney. She was born shortly after the Civil War to John Todd Mahorney and Ann Elizabeth Gray Mahorney, who resided in their business at 28 North Illinois Street. Her father was the proprietor of an ornamental hair (wig) store in downtown Indianapolis. Also, he was a community activist associated with the Negro convention movement and the labor movement that fought for African

Fig. 7.5 Gertrude Amelia Mahorney, first black graduate of Butler University. Courtesy of Special Collections, Butler University Libraries.

American inclusion within the ranks of local unions. He valued education and fine culture and was a member of the Association of Western Writers, a literary organization founded in Indiana in 1885, dedicated to the writers of verse and general literature and the advancement of the fine arts.[5]

The first foreign language taught in Indianapolis public schools was German because many of the early German immigrants regarded the Indianapolis Public School System to be inferior, with too much emphasis placed on religion, and believed that their children would be better educated in the German language. In 1869, with the insistence of the politically powerful German community, all public schools were required to offer German if twenty-five parents requested it.

Gertrude Amelia Mahorney was raised in the household of her maternal grandmother, Johanna Gray, a Prussian, who spoke German and provided an environment in which Gertrude became proficient in the language. Her family held membership in the Christ Church Episcopal Cathedral, on the Governor's Circle (modern day Monument Circle), where few upper-class African Americans attended.

In 1877, she traveled with her family to England to study for a year and lived in London's East End; there she had the opportunity to interact with people of diverse backgrounds. She was the first identifiable African American to graduate from Butler University (fig. 7.5), and she received her Bachelor of Arts in German in 1887 and her Master of Arts in German in 1889.

Her translations of news stories from German to English appeared in Indianapolis newspapers, and she taught in German at the colored public schools, School 23 and School 24. She briefly relocated to Pittsburgh, Pennsylvania, and taught in a colored school, then returned to Indianapolis and was unable to secure a permanent teaching position. The schools' reluctance to hire her may have been retaliatory, connected to the civil rights and union participation of her father. Later, she accepted a teaching position at the Ohio Street Colored School in Rockville, Indiana.

African Americans of the late nineteenth century were greatly indebted to the aforementioned pioneers in education: Samuel Smothers, Nancy Smothers, William David McCoy, and Gertrude Mahorney. Only a few decades earlier, slaves had been prohibited from learning to read and write. Slave owners believed that slaves who could read literature such as the Bible and the US Constitution may be more determined to fight for their freedom. Many slaves caught learning to read and write were either beaten mercilessly or killed for this transgression.

These Black pioneers of education dedicated their lives to uplift their community by providing institutions wherein African Americans could learn to

Fig. 7.6 Major Taylor, internationally known bicyclist. Drawing by Shonna Jennings.

read and write. The public school system opened a new vista for students to explore and to expand their intellectual horizons. Armed with their education, they were encouraged to read books and newspapers and feel a sense of pride when Blacks were prominently featured. One newspaper article piqued their interest and made them feel proud members of the Indianapolis community. Many opined that if this athlete could be so successful in his sport, then perhaps they could be successful in other aspects of life. The series motivated them to read and expand their intellectual horizons. The featured sports hero was Major Taylor.

Marshall Walter "Major" Taylor was born on November 26, 1878, to Gilbert Taylor, a Civil War veteran who fought with the Twenty-Eighth Regiment Indiana Infantry (Colored), and Saphronia Kelter Taylor in Bucktown, in the western quadrant of Indianapolis primarily occupied by African Americans. His father was employed as a coachman for the Southards, a prominent white family that had historical roots in Greencastle, Indiana.

Through the employment of his father, Marshall befriended Daniel Southard, who was the same age. They became fast friends, and the Southards, during a time of intense racial discrimination, recognized the sincerity of their friendship and wanted to raise them together.

From the age of eight until the age of twelve, Taylor lived with the Southards and received the same advantages afforded their son in reference to fine clothing, warm meals, and excellent education. Unfortunately, in 1890, this relationship abruptly ended when the Southards relocated to Chicago.

Daniel Southard was fond of riding his bicycle through the neighborhood, so his parents bought Taylor his first bicycle so that he could join the fun. Taylor became so proficient as a rider, doing clever tricks for children in the neighborhood, that Tom Hay, a local bicycle shop owner, hired him to perform stunts in front of the store to increase sales. He received the moniker "Major" because he performed while dressed in a Union soldier's uniform.

As a teenager and avid sports aficionado, Taylor competed in many local bicycle races and, because of the social climate of the day, encountered overt racism on many occasions. In 1893, he competed in a race, broke a track record, and was insulted with racist epithets from the crowd. Ultimately, he was barred from the track and admonished to never return. The following year, he set a world record during a championship race sponsored by the Capital City Track, and the next day the track instituted a whites-only policy.

In the early 1890s, Taylor was employed by the Harry T. Hearsey bicycle shop, and he later met Louis "Birdie" Munger, owner of the Munger Cycle Manufacturing Company. Munger relocated to the East Coast and established the Worcester Cycle Manufacturing Company in Worcester, Massachusetts. He hired Taylor as an advertisement consultant who visited high schools and colleges to promote the company's bicycles.

In 1896, Taylor was crowned as one of the top racers in America (fig. 7.6), and he debuted his professional career and participated in an indoor track event at Madison Square Garden, New York, in front of five thousand screaming bicycle fans. As his celebrity and fame in the racing circles increased, he competed in Canada, Denmark, Germany, England, France, and Australia. President Theodore Roosevelt was one of his most ardent supporters, keeping track of Taylor's exploits throughout his career, which spanned two decades.

The final days of Major Taylor's life were unfortunate. His marriage dissolved, he suffered from bad investments, and he developed serious medical issues. On June 21, 1932, he died penniless in the charity ward of the Cook County Hospital in Chicago, Illinois.[6]

EIGHT

POWER OF THE FOURTH ESTATE

APPROACHING THE TURN OF THE twentieth century, African Americans adopted the adage of English author Edward Bulwer-Lytton and agreed that "the pen is mightier than the sword." They understood that a progressive, upwardly mobile citizenry required a powerfully dynamic press in order to promote, energize, and organize the community and keep them abreast of newsworthy events. Also, they acknowledged the power of the press to initiate change and its importance in their journey toward freedom and equality. The press was an important weapon that they could employ in their war against exclusion and disenfranchisement. In the January 7, 1899, edition of the *Indianapolis Recorder,* beneath the title and above the masthead were the solemn words "A Negro Newspaper devoted to the best interests of the colored people of Indiana."

The history of African Americans in Indianapolis after the Civil War was documented by several African American newspapers whose primary objective was, in the words iconic broadcast journalist Edward R. Murrow, to "illuminate rather than agitate."[1] During this period, many African Americans experienced the painful discrimination instituted by northern-born southern sympathizers in government and in the general Indianapolis population.

Angered by the outcome of the Civil War, these southern sympathizers sought avenues to express their outrage and denied basic rights and privileges to African Americans. Union soldiers took precautions to ensure the safety of former slaves from white hostility and backlash. In essence, the newspapers strove to organize and galvanize the grass roots and put African Americans on a trajectory of upward social mobility to help them become more socially acceptable and less threatening to their white counterparts in Indianapolis.

Fig. 8.1 George Pheldon Stewart, founder of the *Indianapolis Recorder*.
Courtesy of Indiana Historical Society.

The *Indianapolis Leader*, founded by brothers Benjamin, Robert, and James Bagby and published in 1879, was the first African American newspaper in Indianapolis. The *Indianapolis Colored World*, founded by Edward E. Cooper and Edwin F. Horn in 1883, and the *Indianapolis Freeman*, founded by George Knox in 1884, were the most historically significant in that they covered international and national news whereas the *Indianapolis Leader* focused primarily on local and societal news. The *Indianapolis Recorder*, founded by George P. Stewart (fig. 8.1) and William H. Porter in 1895, began as a two-page church bulletin and turned into a four-page newspaper that exhorted African Americans to be moral, to be proud of their racial and cultural heritage, and to combat stereotypes. The *Recorder* featured excerpts of popular sermons and biographical sketches with a moral focus. The paper instilled a great deal of pride in the local African American population, many of whom were former slaves from southern states.[2]

The reporting formats of the *Indianapolis Colored World* and the *Freeman* were quite similar in that these weeklies regularly covered topics concerning internationally and nationally known political and religious leaders. Also covered were the burgeoning African American colleges of the South and their contributions to the betterment of the race. Articles concerning Rust College of Holly Springs, Mississippi; Morris Brown College of Atlanta, Georgia; and Knoxville College of Knoxville, Tennessee, appeared frequently.

In addition to these more academic and cerebral topics, there were a host of herbal remedies and elixirs, department-store fashions, and skin-lightening and hair-straightening advertisements. One major factor that differentiated the *Freeman* from the *Indianapolis Colored World* was that the latter had a section dedicated to national and local entertainment. Many of the late-nineteenth-century editions contained advertisements for the Gideon's Minstrel Carnival, Professor G. W. Housley's Grand Concert Band, Ernest Hogan's Funny Folks presenting "A Country Coon," and Bob Cole and Billy Johnson's presentation "A Trip to Coon Town."[3]

Concerning more serious, culturally enlightening entertainment, the January 20, 1901, edition of the *Colored World* covered the appearance of the Canadian Jubilee Singers and Imperial Orchestra at Allen Chapel African Methodist Episcopal (AME) Church, which had a twenty-cent admission. Also, the April 30 edition covered the appearance of the "Famous Black Patti Troubadours," headed by Madame Sissieretta Jones, the greatest singer of her race. Jones, whose stage name was Black Patti in honor of the Italian-French internationally acclaimed operatic soprano Adelina Patti, had appeared at the Washington Theatre on Indiana Avenue in the late 1890s. She also sang for four consecutive US presidents: Benjamin Harrison, Grover Cleveland, William McKinley, and Theodore Roosevelt."[4]

The *Indianapolis Recorder* was an influential force in the African American fine arts community. In the early 1900s, many articles featured Henry Hart and

Fig. 8.2 Henry Hart, musician who played for a president and governors. Drawing by
Shonna Jennings.

Fig 8.3 Myrtle Hart, accomplished harpist. Drawing by Shonna Jennings.

their musical performances around the city and country. In the May 17, 1902, edition, an article reported, "Miss Myrtle Hart attendance at Theodore Drury's production of Faust at New York last week. . . . Miss Myrtle Hart, harpist, who has made for herself a reputation equaled by few came from Indianapolis to attend the opera."[5] In the February 27, 1904, edition, an article highlighted a

Fig. 8.4 Hazel Hart-Hendricks, musician and Indianapolis schoolteacher. Drawing by Shonna Jennings.

sacred concert at the Flanner Guild given by the Allen African-Methodist Episcopal choir: "The fashionable vaudeville given by Mrs. Henry Hart and Mrs. A. E. Allen promises to be one of the treats of the season." The African American press legitimized the notion that a certain segment of its community enjoyed the finer aspects of fine arts entertainment. Perhaps this was another indication of the community's willingness to ingratiate itself with similar segments of the majority community?[6]

Henry Hart (fig. 8.2), a nationally renowned African American violinist and composer, performed at Allen Chapel AME Church in the late 1890s. He performed for President Benjamin Harrison and several Indiana governors. Myrtle Hart (fig. 8.3), his daughter whom he trained as a harpist, was described by the *Indianapolis Colored World* as "the only colored harpist in the country."[7]

Hazel Hart-Hendricks (8.4), his second daughter and a music teacher, was a 1930–1931 graduate of Butler University. She was an assistant principal at Indianapolis Public School 37 in 1927 and was promoted to principal shortly thereafter. She taught music, endorsed manual training and domestic science, and encouraged children to participate in all aspects of art. In 1935, she was killed in a car/bus accident while returning with her students from an engagement in Frankfort, Indiana. The school was named in her honor.[8]

In spite of the fact that less than several decades earlier Blacks had been prohibited from acquiring permanent residency in the state and subjected to a stifling social climate replete with remnants of the antebellum South, a few Blacks prospered economically. During the middle to late nineteenth century, while African Americans were gaining a foothold in commerce in Indianapolis, as evidenced by the economic success of the Smotherses and their enterprising daughter, Hortense, they were making advancements in politics and government as well.

NINE

THE TWENTIETH CENTURY

Going "Up South"

AFTER THE CIVIL WAR, MANY former slaves left the South in search of better living conditions in which to raise their families. They were made aware of employment opportunities that were unimaginable in the South. Many jubilantly declared upon their departure, that they were going North from the South, hence the expression "up South." The transition from the nineteenth to the twentieth century in Indianapolis was characterized by feelings of conquest, civil protest, and celebration. The Spanish-American War of 1898, in which America was victorious, had just ended. It had been fought over Spanish colonial rule and economic expansion in the Americas and the United States' wish for economic expansion abroad. Future president Theodore Roosevelt led his troops up San Juan Hill in victory in what proved to be one of the most iconic, historically memorable events of that war. Interestingly, although African American soldiers from the US Tenth Cavalry, called the Buffalo Soldiers, also fought and died for the interests of America, they received scant, abbreviated articles in US newspapers. Buffalo Soldiers from Indianapolis were among the casualties of war.

In Indianapolis, this topic generated heated debates among African Americans, many of whom felt that America had not lived up to its ideals of freedom, justice, and equality and that Black soldiers should not shed blood on battlefields for America. Why should we fight for a country that has no compassion for our people? Why should we protect the time-honored values of American democracy if they are not extended to us? How can we fight to empower our communities and be recognized as bona fide American citizens? Are we stooges for the majority community, willing to shed our blood on the battlefield for American democracy and then return "home" to be treated like second-class citizens? These questions dominated political and social discourse. The March 18, 1898, edition of the *Indianapolis Freeman* editorialized: "If the government wants our support and services, let us demand and get a guarantee for our safety and protection at home. When we are guaranteed freedom and equality before the law, as other American citizens, then we will have the right, as such, to take up arms in defense of our country." Indianapolis Buffalo Soldiers included Private James W. Gibson, Private John C. Howerton, and Private John Smith. Two decades later, during World War I, Crispus Attucks High School educator, civil rights activist, and attorney Dr. John Morton-Finney was a member of the Buffalo Soldiers.

The early years of the twentieth century in Indianapolis saw an influx of African Americans, many of whom were former slaves, from southern states, most notably Mississippi, Tennessee, and Kentucky. Many were in need of social services, requiring housing, health, employment, and education. The Flanner House, a social service agency established in 1898 by Francis Flanner, provided these services in a large, rectangular wooden building on the corner of Rhode Island Avenue and Blake Street, less than a block from Indiana Avenue. Many of the recently arrived former slaves receiving services there flocked to the small entertainment venues along Indiana Avenue to enjoy the music of itinerant musicians and entertainers.

In 1904, the World's Fair opened in Saint Louis to the delight of millions of Americans and citizens from around the world. Because that city is close to Indianapolis, much of the excitement, glitz, and glamour of the international event traveled northward and enlivened the entertainment scene on Indiana Avenue. The World's Fair focused on race, empire, industry, and entertainment and provided an interesting segue to events on Indiana Avenue. Indianapolis AfricanAmericans were exposed to new ideas in business, commerce, and industry as illustrated by the exhibits of the World's Fair. Many felt empowered by these ideas and believed that they could incorporate them into their communities and improve their positions in life. Much of the information gleaned from African Americans in neighboring states encouraged the Black citizenry of Indianapolis to struggle harder for freedom and justice.

Near the second decade of the twentieth century, as African Americans entered the city before World War I, they brought from the South an entertainment tradition that they longed to preserve and celebrate:

> These newcomers brought folklore and tall tales that they were eager to share with their northern neighbors, as well as anyone else who might listen. They brought a desire to amuse them and relive the few

fond memories they cherished of the South. Perhaps it was the cheerful memory of a slave wedding, when the bride and groom would jump over a broom indicating the union of two souls, or the birth of a baby, when at midnight with the stars ablaze, its tiny body was lifted toward the heaven by strong, callused, black hands and the words declared, "Behold, the only thing greater than yourself."[1]

They searched for a welcoming community where they could kick up their heels and be entertained. Many flocked to Indiana Avenue to visit its entertainment venues of various genres, including ragtime, family bands, blues dance halls, minstrelsy, and vaudeville.

The entertainment community was blessed with the appearance of Noble Sissle. Being the son of a minister and school teacher from an upper-middle-class family and a college student, he distinguished himself in the entertainment community by performing in previously segregated venues.

The theatrical section of the February 23, 1918, edition of the *Indianapolis Freeman* contained a story about Noble Sissle, an up-and-coming vocalist, composer, lyricist, bandleader, and playwright. Sissle was born in Indianapolis on July 10, 1889, to Reverend George A. Sissle and Martha Angeline Scott-Sissle. He attended Butler College (Butler University) and wrote the fight song "Butler Will Shine Tonight," which is still performed during athletic events.

During World War I, Sissle was stationed in France as a sergeant drum major in the Thirteenth New York Infantry. He wrote in the *Indianapolis Freeman*, "My chief duty is singing and producing amusement for the boys.... Lieutenant Jim Europe is with the company; he also is in good spirits. In fact, the whole bunch ... is in a fine mood ... the French are very appreciative and polite."[2]

In the January 31, 1920, edition of the *Indianapolis Freeman*, this article appeared:

There are few of us who will not forget the late Lieutenant James Reese Europe and his famous "Hell Fighters" (306th Infantry) Band which only a few months ago were the talk of this country and Europe. In that renowned aggregation was Lieutenant Noble Lee Sissle, the celebrated lyric tenor, who was the business partner and co-star of the eminent music director. Throughout the country, Sissle's fame preceded him and the critics heralded his coming with great praise. Of course, Lieutenant Europe and the band set the whole America to reeling and rocking in delight of the wonderful melodies. But this Lieutenant Sissle seemed to shine above it all with his appealing lyrical voice. There was a passionate tone in his voice of song that pierced the heart of hundreds here and thousands in France wherever he sang. There were those of us who heard him sing long before the war, way back in the old Hoosier capitol of Indiana, but never as he sang since the war. There was a new appeal in his notes: a sort of a pleading note of the love-lorn and then the happy finishing melody of the conqueror.[3]

Many African American citizens were proud of the exploits of Noble Sissle both at home in Indianapolis and abroad.

TEN

FRANCIS "FRANK" FLANNER

THE 1900 CENSUS RECORDED 15,931 Blacks in Indianapolis out of a total population of 169,164; they made up roughly 9 percent of the population. Intermittent waves of Black migrants were attracted to the city by gainful (albeit menial) employment, decent living conditions, and better educational opportunities than the southern states provided. Unfortunately, once they arrived, their survival was in jeopardy because no governmental agencies or majority organizations were advocating on their behalf.

Many Blacks lived in cramped quarters in shanties that bordered the White River without running water, toilets, and heat. As a consequence of the conditions, there was an outbreak of tuberculosis, and the brunt of the blame was placed on African Americans. A sense of powerlessness pervaded the atmosphere. They considered many questions: How can we survive? Should we return to the South, where we knew our place in society? Have we jumped out of the fire into the proverbial frying pan?

In spite of some negative attitudes toward African Americans, there were several community institutions that welcomed them. These institutions became the bedrock of the burgeoning African American community by providing social services that made the transition from their meager agricultural existence in the South to their urban existence in the North as comfortable as possible. Among one of the first was the Flanner House, established in the late nineteenth century.

It would have been understandable had Francis Flanner ignored the suffering of recently migrated African Americans in Indianapolis. He was member of a prominent white family and enjoyed all the privileges of white citizenship. But deep in his soul he must have adhered to the biblical passage "that which

Fig. 10.1 Francis Flanner. Courtesy of Bruce W. Buchanan.

you do to the least of thy brethren you've done unto me" (Matthew 25:40). Disregarding ill feelings from members of his community, he set out to improve the station of African Americans in Indianapolis. Blacks appreciated his help and felt empowered by having a supporter of his magnitude to aid them in their struggle for justice. What distinguished Francis Flanner from other Indianapolis residents? Did his Christian background influence his charity, or did other factors contribute? Why did he focus on the problems of impoverished African Americans? Did he recognize the relationship between aiding African Americans and empowering the community in future decades?

To understand the social dynamics that molded such a remarkable human being, one must examine the dynamics of his upbringing. Frank William Flanner (fig. 10.1) was born on December 5, 1854, in Mount Pleasant, Ohio, to Henry Beeson Flanner and Orpha Annette Tyler Flanner. His parents married on June 20, 1843, in Henry County, Indiana, and later relocated to Dent County, Missouri, and purchased a large plantation with the hope of establishing a college there. His father was a teacher, farmer, and musician who served as a drum major the Union Army during the Civil War. He died during the war.

His mother was born in 1824 and was educated at the prestigious Miss Axtell's Seminary in New York. After the death of her husband, she moved to Indianapolis in search of better opportunities for her children and sent money to a Missouri lawyer to maintain and pay taxes on the plantation property. The attorney proved to be a person of questionable character and used the money for his personal benefit. He squandered her personal savings, and she was left with only $100 and seven children to feed, shelter, and clothe. Distraught because of her disastrous financial situation, she sought employment immediately. She operated a boarding house near downtown to support her family. She used a portion of her husband's Civil War pension to finance the establishment of a funeral business for her young son Francis.

Mary Hockett, the wife of Frank William Flanner, was born in 1863 to Cyrus W. Hockett and Rebecca J. Hockett in the Quaker village of Plainfield, Indiana. Both were hotel owners. She was a teacher who excelled in dramatic readings and had studied in Boston, New York, Chicago, Cincinnati, and Berlin, Germany. The fact that she was a Quaker may explain her antislavery, abolitionist orientation later in her life. The Flanners had three daughters—Mary Emma, Janet Tyler, and June Hildegarde—whose lives exemplified a quest for justice and dignity for all human beings regardless of race, sex, creed, or color.

Janet Tyler Flanner (fig. 10.2) was born on March 13, 1892, in Indianapolis. Around the turn of the twentieth century, she experienced an event that shaped the philosophy and values of her young life. Booker T. Washington, the famous

Fig. 10.2 Janet Tyler Flanner. Courtesy of Bruce W. Buchanan.

African American educator, orator, author, and adviser to US presidents, was a guest in their home. The local hotels refused service to African Americans regardless of their social station, so Black dignitaries had to find lodging in the local liberal-minded community.

In 1897, one quiet evening in her living room, Janet sat on Washington's lap. She reminisced, "He put his arm around me and said, you're not afraid of me because I'm very, very black." She said, "Why should I be. It makes no difference." She then mused, "I was already a pretty educated child." The night she sat on Washington's lap was exciting. There was a Black servant name Clifton who became angry when he heard that the dinner guest was Black. "Mrs. Flanner," he said, "I'm not going to wait on another black man."[1] Mrs. Flanner told him he could leave. But then Clifton found out that Washington was a famous Black man who had been invited to dinner at the White House. Clifton became curious and decided to stay. Janet's innocent and loving response to Washington and Mrs. Flanner's ultimatum for Clifton spoke volumes about the influence of the Quaker society, with its concern for human dignity and respect for other people, on the Flanner home.

Janet attended the prestigious Tudor Hall (now Park Tudor) and was president of her class from 1905 to 1906. Later, she journeyed to the University of Chicago with the intent of studying literature, or as she termed it "the persuasion of words," but she left abruptly in 1912 after the suicide of her father. It was determined that Frank William Flanner died by suicide with cyanide poisoning. In 1917 near the end of World War I, Janet returned to Indianapolis and was employed as a film critic at the *Indianapolis Star* daily newspaper.

In 1918, Janet briefly married William "Lane" Rehm, whom she met while a student at the University of Chicago, and they divorced on good terms in 1926. She ultimately embraced her natural attraction to women; earlier, she had met Solita Solano in Greenwich Village, New York, and they became lifelong lovers. In 1925, Janet and Solita relocated to Paris, where Janet wrote her first novel, *Cubical City*, which concerned young artists in New York during the Jazz Age. During this time period, Janet wrote extensively to family back in the States concerning her impressions of France from an American perspective. Jane Grant, wife of *New Yorker* editor Harold Ross, recommended that she consider the publication of her letters in the *New Yorker*. She accepted the offer and wrote her column Letter from Paris for almost fifty years.

Although the Flanner family associated with the crème de la crème in the social circles of Indianapolis and attended the Congregational Church on the corner of Sixteenth Street and Delaware Street, the members were concerned with the downtrodden in the city. Among their friends were esteemed citizens like Colonel Eli Lilly, who founded the pharmaceutical giant the Eli Lilly Company; Booth Tarkington, novelist and dramatist; Kurt Vonnegut Sr., architect and partner in the Vonnegut and Bohn architecture firm; and Albert Lieber, the millionaire owner of a brewery.

It is apparent that the Quaker and Congregational churches helped to shape the norms and mores of the Flanner family. Their influence somewhat explains Frank William Flanner's motivation to establish the Flanner House to aid the downtrodden of society. Witnessing the influx of African Americans beset with a multitude of problems, Flanner took action. He could have easily disregarded the plight of struggling former slaves who migrated to Indianapolis, but he rolled up his sleeves to help the most oppressed and despised of his community. That was Francis William "Frank" Flanner.[2]

WHITE POLICEMEN MURDERED!
WHERE'S JESSE COE?

ALTHOUGH THE MAJORITY OF BLACKS who migrated to Indianapolis from the South desired to be law-abiding citizens, earn the respect of their white counterparts, and live in harmony, a few brought criminal behavior to the city and caused problems for the general Black citizenry. One of the most sensational news stories to rock the early twentieth century was the murder of two white Indianapolis policemen by two African American men. Questions about this newsworthy event undoubtedly troubled the Black community: Would it adversely affect their march toward freedom and acceptance? Would they face political repercussions as a consequence of this sensational event? Would the entire African American community by blamed for the actions of two individuals?

The event began on a chilly, damp night on September 30, 1904, and it would intensify the racial animosity between the African American and white communities of Indianapolis for many years. The principals involved were Jesse Coe and George Williams, childhood friends from the small town of Coe Ridge, Kentucky, who had recently relocated to Indianapolis, and Charles J. Russell and Edward J. Petticord, Caucasian patrolmen for the Indianapolis Police Department. William Lynwood Montell, department head of Folk and Intercultural Studies at the University of Western Kentucky, recorded the incident in his book, *The Saga of Coe Ridge: A Study in Oral History*. He recounts that two policemen responded to a call that concerned two drunken Negroes reportedly fighting on the corner of Twenty-Fourth Street and Indianapolis Avenue. When the policemen arrived, they observed two men quietly talking to each other in an alley behind a house located at 2336 Indianapolis Avenue. William Jackson, an acquaintance of both men, overheard them say that they "had a job on." In the street vernacular of the day, that meant they were planning a robbery.

Fig. 11.1 *Left,* Charles J. Russell, murdered police officer.
Fig. 11.2 *Right,* Edward J. Petticord, murdered police officer.

As the policemen approached the men to question them, Coe placed his hand inside his suit jacket and shirt, and the police officer, Charles J. Russell, nervously asked him what he was hiding. Suddenly, Coe pulled out a revolver and immediately shot and killed Patrolman Russell (fig. 11.1). Coe quickly departed, with Patrolman Petticord (fig. 11.2) in hot pursuit, and as Petticord ran past Williams, Williams shot Petticord in the back. He died on October 2, 1906.

Word of the policemen's deaths spread quickly throughout Indianapolis, and an intensive dragnet was organized to capture the killers and bring them to justice. One of the gun that fired the fatal bullets was owned by George Williams (fig. 11.3), and he was subsequently apprehended, convicted, and hanged in the Michigan City Penitentiary on February 8, 1907.

Jesse Coe eluded the police dragnet, went to his sister's home near the banks of Fall Creek, and spent the night hidden under the floorboards in her kitchen. The next morning, he dressed himself as an elderly lady with a bonnet, long dress, and cane and walked to the Union Station in downtown Indianapolis, where he boarded a train to return to Coe Ridge. Back in the Kentucky hills of his youth, Coe hid in a friend's barn and then lived in a cave for months.

Chief Robert Metzger of the Indianapolis Police Department approved the establishment of a $1,500 bounty for the apprehension and conviction of Coe, and the news of this bounty was circulated throughout the United States on

Fig. 11.3 Mug shot of George Williams. Courtesy of Indiana Archives & Records Administration.

wanted posters with a photograph of Coe (fig. 11.4). His friend and distant relative Claude Anders considered the enormity of the bounty and collaborated with the Monroe County (Kentucky) Sheriff's Department in an attempt to apprehend Coe and obtain the reward.

On August 8, 1908, a scheme was devised wherein Coe and Anders would go squirrel hunting and at a designated location the police would attempt an apprehension. The sheriff's posse hid in the thickets, and at a given time, Anders was directed to holler, "Squirrel up in the tree," then walk around the tree and duck for cover. As the scheme commenced, Coe lifted his shotgun toward the tree as if to shoot the squirrel, and members of the posse stepped out from behind trees and shrubbery. They opened fire from all barrels of their shotguns and killed Coe instantly.

A youngster from Coe Ridge saw the wagon that was carrying the body of Jesse Coe to Tompkinsville, ran to Coe Ridge, and informed the residents of his murder. Within an hour, Coe Ridge residents with pistols and rifles hurried to Tompkinsville to exact revenge. By the time they arrived, the train had departed the station en route to Indianapolis, and the angry crowd returned to Coe Ridge without firing a shot.[1]

On arrival, Jesse Coe's body was embalmed at the Willis Mortuary, located near Indiana Avenue. In accordance with the directives of the Indianapolis

$1,500.00 REWARD

FOR

JESSE COE=Negro

*Wanted for Murder of Police Officer Chas. Russell,
on Night of September 30, 1906*

DESCRIPTION: 32 years old, about 5 feet 6 inches, 140
to 150 pounds, Brown Skin, Smooth Face when last seen,
High Cheek Bones, Scrofula Scar about two inches long on
left side of neck near jaw. Employed as farm-hand, also as
laborer sewer and construction work. Is native of Kentucky.

WIRE ALL INFORMATION TO

ROBERT METZGER, Indianapolis, Ind.
CHIEF OF POLICE

JESSE COE·ALIAS COLE

Fig. 11.4 Wanted poster for Jesse Coe.

Police Department, it was transported to the department's courtyard, where it was put on public display for several days. The coffin was placed against a wall in an upright position, and spectators viewed the body as if Coe stood on his feet. The following account was reported in the August 27, 1908, edition of the *Indianapolis Sun*:

> The body lay in state until two o'clock when it was sent to the home of Mrs. Cassie Raspberry of 1031 Coe Street near City Hospital. Mrs. Raspberry went to the police headquarters and identified the body as that of her brother and said she would take charge of it.
>
> The Negro undertaker, whom she had employed, made arrangements to take charge of the body as soon as police were through with it. . . . The most gruesome spectacle in the history of the city was witnessed Thursday when fully twenty-five thousand people, men, women and children viewed the body of Coe as he lay in a cheap pine coffin in the courtyard at police headquarters . . . they passed by the coffin at the rate of ninety-four (people) a minute.

The *Sun* reported that "the corpse of the small Black man lay in the plainest sort of coffin pipe box (fig. 11.5). The shirt was thrown open so that the spectators might see the wound just below the heart caused by the bullet from the Kentucky sheriff's rifle."[2] The funeral service was held at the Antioch Baptist Church at 2:00 p.m. Monday, August 31, 1908, and his body was transported by train to Tompkinsville, Kentucky, where a service was held before interment in the Coe Ridge Cemetery.

Fig 11.5 Jesse Coe in casket. Drawing by Shonna Jennings.

Claude Anders, the distant relative and betrayer of Coe, was paid $600, escorted to the train station by an Indianapolis police detective, and quietly returned to Kentucky. Later, Anders declared that "he would have turned Coe over sooner to the police department had it not been that on the night Patrolmen Russell and Petticord were killed that he (Anders) was locked up and held for several days in jail. He said the police did not treat him right."[3] Concerning the sincerity of Anders's statement, the Monroe County Sheriff's Department responded in the August 29 edition of the *Sun*, "Anders would have been alright, said Deputy Sheriff Conklin of Kentucky, 'If he hadn't got to drinking whisky and playing nigger. Of course, he had to tell everything he knew and those niggers would have killed him.'"[4]

TWELVE

MADAM C. J. WALKER AND EARLY AFRICAN AMERICAN FEMALE TRAILBLAZERS

ALTHOUGH AFRICAN AMERICANS RECOGNIZED THE importance of community organization and cohesion to attempts to become empowered and claim bona fide American citizenship and respect, several divisive issues bubbled below the surface. Two of these issues—colorism and classism—developed during slavery, arising from the dynamics of the relationships between owners and slaves, and were transported to Indianapolis along the Underground Railroad.

Generally, on slave plantations in the South, there were at least two distinct, identifiable slave classes. The first, the "house Negro," in many instances, was light complexioned, biracial, and the offspring of the slave master. He or she lived in the plantation house, did menial chores, and received preferential treatment because of his or her biological relationship to the slave master.

The second, the "field Negro," was darker complexioned and may have been the biological offspring of the slave master but phenotypically was African American. He or she lived in the slave quarters, worked the fields day and night, and fed from the troughs of swine and other farm animals. He or she was severely beaten for the slightest infraction and was required to be docile to the point of being infantile.

"House Negroes" worked tirelessly to match the general comportment of the slave master. They walked and talked like him and, in some instances, adopted his rationale for the institution of slavery. They were privileged, and they refused to be identified with the "field Negroes," developing a socially rigid caste system that excluded them. "House Negroes" adopted the religion of the slave master, which in many cases was the Baptist religion, and demonstrated how devoted they were to the Christian scripture that justified their involuntary servitude.

"Field Negroes" maintained, to some degree, their ancestral connection to Africa. They did not reverently embrace the religion of their slave masters. Unbeknownst to the slave master, they stole away to the deep forest at night and practiced religious ceremonies derived from West Africa. These ceremonies were based on African spirits and were later referred to as Voodoo or Hoodoo.

When these two distinct classes of slaves migrated to Indianapolis during the post–Civil War period, they brought their "slavery baggage" with them. Some former members of the "house Negro" category desired to maintain social distance from their "field Negro" counterparts. Many of the "house Negroes" received better education during the post-slavery period and attended colleges in the North.[1] In Indianapolis, this historical phenomenon resulted in the separation of the race and societal disorganization. Interestingly, many of the socially mobile male members of the "house Negro" category attended more mainstream denominations, such as Baptist, Methodist, or Presbyterian. Members of the "field Negro" category more often attended the charismatic churches whose beliefs were based on the spiritualism transported on slave ships to America during the Middle Passage.[2]

At the turn of the twentieth century, there was a mechanism in place that assigned certain Blacks to various societal categories. Variables like education, skin color, hair texture, years removed from slavery, and civility determined which rung an African American would occupy on the societal ladder. Humorously, there developed a small Black upper class that appeared to be a comically buffoonish imitation of the Indianapolis white aristocracy. In essence, their dress, mannerisms, lifestyle, speech patterns, and general comportment were crafted to be as closely associated with the majority community as possible.

Among the leading Black aristocratic families were the Venables, Thorntons, Bagbys, Elberts, Hills, Furnises, McCoys, Christys, and Knoxes. The majority of these families were associated with Bethel AME, Second Baptist, and Jones Tabernacle AME Zion Churches, and they took special measures to ensure that they would not be mistaken for the uneducated, recently migrated Blacks from the South.

Simultaneously, there was a group of upper-class, well-educated African Americans who were as cultured and as civil as the aforementioned group but who maintained their connection to their culture and the less fortunate in the African American community. Individuals like George and Mary E. Cable, Ada Harris, and Emma McCann DuValle came to the aid of the downtrodden on many occasions.

Ada Harris demonstrated the love of her people and acknowledged the history of slavery and the detrimental effects it had on Black people. As a testament to her refusal to surrender her history and culture to the European-mimicking, African American, upwardly mobile, pretentious Black bourgeoisie social class, even her culinary practices spoke volumes. As Earline Rae Ferguson states in her 1997 Indiana University doctoral dissertation entitled "A Community Affair: African-American Women's Club Work in Indianapolis (1879–1917)," which documents the history of African American women's social clubs at the turn of the twentieth century: "Race pride was also manifested in other ways. For instance, the selection and preparation of food gave some club women like Harris an opportunity to revisit the old cultural practices that were challenged by the new way. Most women, when clubs met at their homes, served club sandwiches and tea cakes: Harris cooked chittlins, greens and cracklin' bread."[3] For one afternoon club meeting at Harris' house, she prepared chitlins, collard greens, and hot water corn bread for her socially mobile, bourgeoisie friends. She watched from her living room window as the women approached with frowns and wrinkled noses at the down-home odors that escaped from her kitchen. After the greetings and pleasantries were exchanged, the women met, held their meeting, discussed important topics, and partook of the food. After the departure of these fine, highly cultured ladies of society, Harris noticed that there was not a chitlin left in the pot, a collard green on the serving plate, or a crumb of her corn bread on the plate. These women reconnected with their slavery past, unbuttoned their belts, kicked up their heels, and enjoyed that fine food![4]

Through the guilds and missions of their churches, these social clubs helped organize mutual aid and protection societies for the migrants who were constantly entering the city. These organizations were very important to the vitality of the less fortunate residents of Indianapolis.

As weary Black souls reached the outskirts of Indianapolis from all points South and headed toward Indiana Avenue and Bucktown in search of a roof over their heads and vittles to fill their empty stomachs, they must have desired entertainment. After all, they had just completed a long, tiring trek to the big city and certainly needed an escape from reality to rejuvenate their exhausted spirits. Perhaps a drink, a conversation with folks from "home," and a song from an itinerant banjo player would be a salve for the soul.

For decades, Indiana Avenue patrons frequented modestly appointed entertainment establishments like the Hortense, Pioneer, and Famous Theaters, 513 Indiana Avenue, the Washington Theatre, 521 Indiana Avenue, and the Hill's Indiana Theatre, 412 Indiana Avenue. Patrons took for granted their Spartan accommodations and did not have a choice because many downtown Indianapolis theaters were racially segregated. Along came Madam C. J. Walker, and things changed drastically.

Fig. 12.1 Madam C. J. Walker, African American beauty-culture millionaire. Courtesy of A'Lelia Bundles.

Madam C. J. Walker (fig. 12.1), born Sarah Breedlove on December 23, 1867, in Delta, Louisiana, rose from the cotton fields of the old South and became one of the wealthiest women of any color in America during the early twentieth century. As a young adult living in Saint Louis, she suffered dermatological problems related to baldness, acute dandruff, and the growth of hair. In 1903, as an agent employed by an African American hair-care businesswoman named Annie Malone, Sarah developed her own hair treatment products that addressed these issues. In 1905, her employment prompted her to move to Denver, Colorado, and the following year, she married Charles Joseph Walker and became Madam C. J. Walker. In 1910, she moved to Indianapolis and founded the Madam C. J. Walker Manufacturing Company. Being a wealthy African American woman during this period did not immunize her from racism and discrimination.[5]

Longtime Indiana Avenue resident and historian Tom Ridley, whose parents were contemporaries of Madam Walker and her attorney Freeman Briley Ransom, when asked about Madam Walker, made reference to the book by her great-granddaughter, A'Lelia Bundles, *On Her Ground: The Life and Times of Madam C. J. Walker.*

> Less than a week after the Spencer recital Madam Walker arrived at the Isis Theatre in downtown Indianapolis prepared for a Saturday afternoon of fun. But when she presented her dime admission fee, the ticket agent refused to accept her money, informing her that "colored people" were now required to pay "twenty-five cents." In response to her demand for an explanation of the new policy, the young box office attendant replied that she had received "orders to charge colored persons twenty-five cents each for tickets." An irate Madam Walker insisted that Ransom take action against the theatre. In his formal complaint to the Marion County Court, he demanded $100 in damages for his "clean, sober, neat and orderly" client, who had faced racial discrimination in a public place. No document showing the disposition of the case exists in court records, but the incident surely added to Madam Walker's impatience with Indianapolis and increased her desire to move.[6]

Perhaps, at that moment, she envisioned the construction of an awe-aspiring edifice, more luxuriously appointed than any downtown theater, a place where African Americans would be received with respect and dignity. Madam C. J. Walker died on May 25, 1919, at her country home in Irvington-on-the Hudson, New York, and never saw the beautiful edifice that she envisioned.[7]

On Monday, December 26, 1927, the headlines of the *Indianapolis Recorder* announced the grand opening of the Walker Theatre. It towered majestically

Fig. 12.2 Madam Walker in her Waverly Electric Car. Courtesy of A'Lelia Bundles.

over all edifices on Indiana Avenue. The adoring, appreciative audience saw the Hollywood motion picture *The Magic Flame*, which starred Ronald Colman and Vilma Banky; *The American Beauty*, which starred Billy Dove; and *East Side-West Side*, which starred George O'Brien and Virginia Valli. The live-performance portion of the program featured the Chicago-based dance act billed Lovey and Shorty, The Two Whirlwinds—one of Chicago's fastest dancing acts—and Drake and Walker, dancing duet. Later, the Walker Theatre featured the Cyclonic Jazz Band, the Zulu Jazz Band, and the stage play *Clarence Muse and the Chocolate Dandies*. The Hollywood motion pictures were *Gancho*, with Douglas Fairbanks, and *Get Your Man*, with Clara Bow. The theater boasted the release of the first "100% Talky, All Negro Cast '*Hearts in Dixie*' and the first live appearance of '*Deacon Hampton's Piccaninny Band*' directly from Georgia." Reginald DuValle and his Blackbyrds was the premiere orchestra to open the Walker Theatre.[8]

The Hill's Indiana Theatre featured the Hollywood motion pictures *Shore Leave*, with Richard Barthlemess, and *Body and Soul*, by the African American producer Oscar Micheaux. Tomlinson Hall, located on the corner of Market and Delaware Streets, was one of a few downtown entertainment establishments that allowed African American patronage. It featured internationally and nationally known acts like the Fletcher Henderson Orchestra from New York, Dippy Miller and His Gang—Fifteen Dancers and Entertainers, and the Whitman Sisters.

The Whitman Sisters were the highest-paid act on the Negro Vaudeville Circuit and one of the longest surviving touring companies. They appeared frequently at the Washington Theatre and were considered by many to be the premiere dancing performers of any color in America. The Hume-Mansur Theatre on the Monument Circle and the Murat Temple hosted Roland Hayes, a lyric tenor considered by many to be the first internationally known African American concert artist. He dazzled audiences in America and abroad with his songs in French, German, and Italian.[9]

Right down the avenue sat the Washington Theatre. It featured live stage vaudeville acts such as Dooley and Dooley and Byrd and Ewing, and the Broadway Theatre featured "Shufflin' Sam from Alabama" and two gigantic Charleston contests. Also, occasionally, the blues stopped by to pay a visit. Ida Cox and Edmonia Henderson performed in many of the entertainment venues on Indiana Avenue, especially and most frequently the Washington Theatre and the Hill's Indiana Theatre. They were favorites to patrons, many of whom had recently migrated from the South. Cox hailed from Georgia but ran away from home and landed in the Midwest, where she performed in minstrel shows. Later, she joined New Orleans entertainment icons bandleader King Oliver and pianist "Jelly Roll" Morton and toured the country. Her signature songs that brought down the house nightly were "Blues Ain't Nothin' But" and "Booze Crazy Man Blues."

Edmonia Henderson, a rotund diva from Kentucky, arrived on Indiana Avenue and kicked up a dust storm of controversy. Apparently, she had had a failed romantic relationship with a light-complexioned African American man and had settled the score in the recording studio. There were pretentious, high-society-minded, lighter-complexioned African Americans who did not want to be associated with their darker-complexioned counterparts, but this was an insignificant number.

Some lighter-complexioned African Americans lived on the fringes of society in poverty along with their darker-complexioned counterparts. Henderson's signature song "Brown-Skin Man" exploited this color difference. The song pitted darker-complexioned African Americans against lighter-complexioned African Americans. Some of the lyrics delivered a comparative study of the alleged virtues and vices of "high yellow" and brown men: "*A high yellow* [man] *will throw you and that ain't all / every night they usually home another mule in your stall / a brown skin man will love you, / will surely treat you right, / a yellow man get twenty-five, he slowly draws up like rice.*" Indeed, Edmonia Henderson was a supremely talented blues singer, albeit a troublemaker and controversial entertainer.

While Ida Cox and Edmonia Henderson wowed blues-crazed patrons on Indiana Avenue, a young lad, James "Yank" Rachell, developed his taste for the blues on a sleepy, West Tennessee farm town called Brownsville. A precocious youngster, he taught himself the rudiments of several instruments, including the mandolin and guitar, as he searched to find his voice in the world of entertainment. By a stroke of luck, he met seasoned bluesmen "Sleepy John" Estes and Hammie Nixon. According to Rachell, "Me and singer/guitarist 'Sleepy John' were stickin' around together and then picked up a harmonica player named Hammie and taught him how to play."[10] The trio performed as a jug band, with homemade instruments like washtubs, spoons, and kazoos, throughout Tennessee and adjoining states for both Black and white audiences. In 1958, Rachell came to Indianapolis with his family and ailing wife, and unfortunately she died three years later. He reconnected with Estes and Nixon, and the trio performed together again at college campuses, concerts, festivals, and coffeehouses throughout the United States and Europe. In the 1990s, Rachell was rediscovered once more, and he performed nightly before adoring fans at the Slippery Noodle, a popular downtown blues club.[11]

THIRTEEN

THE *INDIANAPOLIS RECORDER*, CATALYST FOR CHANGE, AND THE MONSTER MEETINGS AT THE SENATE AVENUE YMCA

DURING THE 1930S AND 1940S, the *Indianapolis Recorder* continued to be one of the most significant and influential voices in the African American community. Reflected on the pages of every edition were news stories that allowed Blacks to evaluate their progress and advancement in the social, political, and economic arenas in Indianapolis as compared to historical events occurring around the world. Numerous outstanding news events, both at home and abroad, shaped African Americans' self-image and showed them how far they still had to go to reach freedom and social acceptance.

Many of these events also galvanized the Black community and made them more determined to demand equality. Events occurring in places such as Africa affected the experiences of African Americans in Indianapolis. Such reports served as a catalyst for local civil rights organizations to develop new strategies to confront racism and oppression. On July 6, 1913, one such catalyst began its operation at the corner of Senate Avenue and Michigan Street: the Senate Avenue Young Men's Christian Association (YMCA).

Amid the celebration experienced by many African Americans in Indianapolis and the area considered its heart, Indiana Avenue, there was an undercurrent of illegal activity. Many of the religious and civic leaders regarded this activity as an impediment in their march toward progress and community acceptance, and they took drastic measures to address this problem. How could they expect to improve their living conditions with these terrible social problems in plain sight? Would the activity widen the schism between the well-to-do African Americans and the lower class who were blamed for the problems? Did these problems arise from the long history of slavery? How could African Americans embrace education as a vehicle for self-improvement?

Conventional wisdom dictated that perhaps an institution established in the community and held in high esteem could help address the problems. This institution was the Senate Avenue YMCA and its Monster Meetings. In retrospect, the founding of this institution had an interesting history replete with community pride.

African American leaders formed the Young Men's Prayer Band in 1900, and it had become a branch of the city YMCA by 1910. Black and white leaders agreed that a permanent neighborhood anchor to the religious community would be necessary if they were to achieve the aforementioned goal of community improvement.[1]

A construction campaign was launched, and Black and white community leaders helped raise funds for a new building, which opened as the Senate Avenue YMCA in 1913. Booker T. Washington, educator and president of Tuskegee Institute, Tuskegee, Alabama, dedicated the building. Faburn DeFrantz was the physical director in 1913 and executive secretary from 1916 to 1951, and the Senate Avenue YMCA became one of the largest Black YMCAs in the United States.[2]

DeFrantz envisioned a Christian religious approach to address the rising crime rate. Realizing that this approach would not solve all of the issues, he was compelled to approach the problem from a different perspective. He envisioned a community organization composed of concerned and dedicated men with unquestionable character, impeccable morals, and serious scholarship, and outstanding community engagement. These men formed the Monster Meetings. The Monster Meetings served as focal points for protest and constituent education. As an arm of the Monster Meetings, the Citizens Committee of One Hundred, with its active subcommittees, scrutinized pending legislation and other city and state activities that were likely to have a negative impact on housing, education, and employment in the Black community. Further, the Monster Meetings played a central role in galvanizing the community around such important issues as the relaxation of racial restrictions at Indiana University, the opening of downtown theaters to African Americans, and the integration of the Indiana High School Athletic Association.

Those at the meetings also considered the preparation of the Anti-Hate Bill that became law in 1947, the employment of Blacks in city administrations, and the preparation of the Anti-Segregation Bill that became law in 1949. Each of these issues was discussed in open forums and reported on by knowledgeable, interested individuals and the appropriate committees. Committee reports were often made directly to the Monster Meeting audiences with the confidence that every organization interested in matters affecting the race was represented there.

Education Secretary Robert W. Starms, in his report *Achieving Christian Social Goals through the Public Forum: An Interpretative Study of the Monster Meeting*, opined, "The Monster Meeting as an institution drew additional strength and support from the community and set out to wage a relentless fight for first class citizenship. Reaction gave a greater courage to the leaders of this program and they realized that the colored citizens of the community must be aroused to a super alertness."[3] Executive Director Faburn DeFrantz stated, "We must not lose hope and we must hold (on) to our faith, for now we must prove our courage if we are to be free."

Many of the Monster Meeting forums held at the Senate Avenue YMCA featured nationally renowned trailblazers in the African American community. The speakers included Paul Robeson, internationally known human rights activist, bass baritone performer on stages around the world, and twice-named consensus All-American football player from Rutgers College; Dr. Percy Julian, a chemist from DePauw University; Countee Cullen, esteemed poet of the Harlem Renaissance; Alain Locke, writer and philosopher of the Harlem Renaissance; J. Ernest Jenkins, physicist; and Hale Woodruff, Indianapolis-born and internationally known artist.[4]

Many citizens believed that one of the solutions to the myriad of problems in the city would be the strengthening of the family unit, and the Monster Meetings strove valiantly to underscore this approach The participants in the Monster Meetings were cognizant of the fact that the majority of factors that led to familial dysfunction were directly related to their horrendous experiences during slavery. Perhaps this was a development of a post-traumatic slave syndrome, a term coined by internationally renowned researcher Joy DeGruy to describe the multigenerational trauma and injustices experienced by African Americans from the dawn of slavery to the recent deaths of Black citizens at the hands of police.

During this pre–Civil War era, slave owners routinely weakened and destroyed the Black family unit by arbitrarily selling family members to distant plantation. Grieving mothers and fathers witnessed the destruction and separation of their family without any power to prohibit it. The parents developed a sense of powerlessness and impotency and incorporated these feelings into their collective psyches. As a result, former slaves brought these dysfunctional psychological issues to Indianapolis, and they were manifested in aberrant familial social interactions. It was imperative that these issues be resolved in order for the family unit to function in a normal and mentally healthy manner.

—ɯ—

THE ROARIN' TWENTIES

THE THIRD DECADE OF THE twentieth century in Indianapolis was unequivocally earthshaking. World War I had ended, and troops returned home victoriously to a grateful America with loyal, flag-waving citizens who appreciated their sacrifices to ensure freedom and democracy. The economy strengthened, and public confidence skyrocketed. This seemingly "cosmic concoction" of events led to a period of American history never before imagined—the Roarin' Twenties. Indianapolis and America found themselves in an almost surreal time wherein norms and mores were tossed aside and a new zest for life was sought. War-weary Americans simply wanted to dismiss the past, kick up their heels, focus on the future, and enjoy both life and entertainment.

Women affectionately labeled "flappers" rushed toward liberation with reckless abandonment. Snazzy short skirts with long drooping blouses and cascading beaded necklaces made the fashion statement of the day. Money flowed like water as crowds packed music halls to listen to a new genre called jazz. Dance crazes like the Charleston and the Black Bottom, which symbolized freedom from convention and a quest for new social experiences, rocked Indianapolis and the nation.

On Indiana Avenue, new nightclubs and juke joints opened their doors, and folks strutted up and down its fancy corridors in a proud parade of peacocks with their multicolored plumage. African American women viewed this celebratory atmosphere from a distance because their position in society did not match that of their white counterparts. Many did not have the financial resources to purchase the stylish clothes or to visit the downtown dance halls. They were concerned with basic necessities like seeking employment and putting food on their tables.

Adding to the good times, the women's suffrage movement birthed in the eighteenth century had gained momentum and realized its goals. The Nineteenth Amendment to the Constitution was ratified, giving women the right to vote. Historically, women had been denied this right, and with their newfound quest for liberation, they demanded a change of course. The Nineteenth Amendment empowered women to demand equal rights with men and exercise this equality at the ballot box. African American women did not join in the celebratory dance with their white counterparts because enactment of the Nineteenth Amendment did not in effect include women of color.[1] Black women would not effectively gain the right to vote until the Voting Rights Act of 1965 was signed by President Lyndon Baines Johnson, guaranteeing African Americans and other minorities that right.

Interestingly, the spirit of good times of this era was counterbalanced by the introduction of Prohibition. This ban on the sale, consumption, production, importation, and transportation of alcoholic beverages was mandated by the Eighteenth Amendment to the US Constitution.

Religious organizations sensed a decline in the country's moral values and rejoiced over the introduction of this measure. Skeptics believed that religious ethics were being forced on Americans, and as a result, they naturally reacting by circumventing the law and conducting business as usual. Organized crime opened illegal distilleries in Indianapolis and throughout the nation to address the needs of a consuming public, and the crime rate increased astronomically.

In the African American community, Prohibition proved to debilitate progress and the march for freedom and equality. Community organizations such as the various churches and the Senate Avenue YMCA had to double their efforts to fight crime. African American community leaders believed that the proliferation of bootleg joints and speakeasies on Indiana Avenue would plunge the community into the depths of illegal business practices and destroy the community.[2] Many African American leaders pondered whether the societal gains of the earlier days of the century would be dashed to bits by Prohibition.

On Indiana Avenue, as the Roarin' Twenties rolled on, many residents were unaware of an underground nefarious movement: the Ku Klux Klan. Organized by disgruntled Confederate soldiers after their defeat during the Civil War, the Ku Klux Klan initially operated by terrorizing African Americans with beatings, lynchings, intimidation, and other acts of terrorism. They hoped that these measures would impede African Americans' march toward liberation and social justice in America and return them to a state of mental servitude.

The Ku Klux Klan was based on white supremacy, white nationalism, and anti-immigration sentiments. In Indianapolis, this organization was spearheaded by

David Curtis Stephenson, a Houston Texan by way of Evansville, who became the grand dragon, or supreme leader of the group.[3] One incident clearly illustrated how Blacks who labored to improve their communities were hoodwinked by majority businesses that did not share their best interests. There were white business establishments that operated in the African American community whose economic viability depended on that community. Apparently, their comportment indicated ulterior motives. Some of these businesses treated their Black customers with dignity and respect during the day and attended racist organization meetings at night.

Madgelyn Hawk, in her book *When the Mourning Dove Cries*, describes the social atmosphere in Indianapolis during this period and an event that involved her family. Unbeknownst to residents of the Indianapolis African American community, there were Ku Klux Klan operatives in their midst. Drake's Markets (fig. 14.1), located at 818–20 West Michigan Street, 1003 North West Street, and 1302–4 North Senate Avenue, in close proximity to Indiana Avenue, was a well-established business in the community owned by Clive and Alma Drake. Its financial viability depended on African American patronage.

Although Drake and his relatives and white merchants greeted customers with kind, warm smiles, nice words, and respect during the day, they religiously attended Ku Klux Klan meetings during the night and were proud participants in its campaign of hate. The *Tolerance* newspaper, Chicago edition of June 6, 1923, displayed the headline "Exposure of 12,208 Ku Klux (Klan) in Marion County Indiana," and among the members were William E. Drake, Ernest Drake, Wilbur Drake, and William W. Drake—all Drake family members.

Interestingly, as if fate and karma had intervened, two decades later, Julia Drake, the daughter of Ku Klux Klan sympathizer Clive Drake, met and fell in love with a young African American man, Richard Emory. He was a handsome, dark-brown man who delivered goods to the market and caught Julia's eye. Secretly, they exchanged information and agreed to rendezvous.

Late one night, Emory ventured into her all-white neighborhood and climbed the latticework to her bedroom, and they had their first romantic encounter. Later, Julia realized that she was pregnant and confided the secret to a cousin, who later told her father. On hearing of his daughter being impregnated by an African American and jeopardizing his social status with the Ku Klux Klan, Clive Drake was outraged and sought a resolution to the problem. The angry father wanted to terminate the pregnancy in order to maintain his position of respect among Ku Klux Klan members.

The daughter delivered a baby girl named Dovey, ran away from home, and went directly to the Emory home for lodging and protection. In hot pursuit, her father and his Ku Klux Klan coconspirators burned a cross on the front lawn.

Fig. 14.1 Drake's Market. Courtesy of Indiana Historical Society.

After a few days, Emory's frightened parents asked her to leave for fear of their lives and the endangerment of their neighbors.

Julia and her baby lived in back alleys behind entertainment venues, abandoned houses, and vacant lots near Indiana Avenue during inclement weather. Breast milk was the baby's only nourishment during this ordeal. The father dispatched his Ku Klux Klan cohorts to find her. Finally, she was captured and returned to her father.

The angry father demanded that she give him custody of the infant and promised to throw the child down a well. Initially, she refused, but he demanded that she sign papers to release the child to his custody or he would be forced to commit her to the "Seven Steeples," the pejorative term for the Central State Mental Hospital.

Finally, she relented, signed the documents, and released the child to the custody of her father. The angry father had a change of heart and gave the child to a prominent, childless African American attorney and his wife—this attorney, a Mr. Wilson, was Clive Drake's personal attorney. The Wilsons raised the child and renamed her Laura. Drake placed his daughter on a bus to Ohio and demanded that she never return.[4]

DAVID CURTIS STEPHENSON AND THE KU KLUX KLAN

IN ITS QUEST FOR EMPOWERMENT and recognition, the African American community encountered substantive obstacles in its march toward societal acceptance and freedom. Aside from racist policies formulated by city government and antagonistic sentiment articulated by some segments of the general community, African Americans in Indianapolis faced external organizations that operated to impede their advancement.

Dismayed, some members of the Black civil rights community anticipated the imminent onslaught of disruptive activity. Intertwined within the fabric of Indianapolis society were threads that were very offensive to African Americans. Restrictions in public accommodation and housing, segregated education, and inadequate medical care became apparent.

African Americans wondered whether the gains accomplished in prior decades would be erased by these internal and external forces. Could neighborhood civil rights organizations counteract this activity? Would the authority of the municipal government supersede the machinations of individuals or organizations that expressed ill will toward Blacks, or would they collaborate? These and other questions perplexed the African American community in Indianapolis during the second decade of the twentieth century. Finally, the answer appeared in Indianapolis in the early 1920s—enter D. C. Stephenson.

During the 1920s, Indianapolis had the unenviable distinction of being one of the most racist cities in America. African Americans constituted 11 percent of the total population, and eight hundred Black students were enrolled in the Indianapolis Public School System. This was a whopping 10 percent increase over the previous decade. Some white citizens were alarmed and took measures to address the situation. Civic organizations popped up all over Indianapolis.

Fig. 15.1 David Curtis Stephenson. Courtesy of Indiana Historical Society.

Daisy Dean Deed and the White Supremacy League, the White People's Protective Association, the Capitol Avenue Protective Association, and the Mapleton Civic Association were some of the most prominent profiled organizations.

In 1925, the governor, the mayor, the majority of the state legislature, and five newly elected members of the school board were either Ku Klux Klan members or sympathizers. As a young man, Indianapolis educator Dr. John Morton-Finney remembered seeing a Klan rally on Meridian Street that lasted for hours as hordes of white-robed, pillowcase-headed Klan members marched defiantly in downtown Indianapolis toward Monument Circle to hold a gigantic rally and recruitment campaign. One of the most prominent planks of their campaign of hate was the insistence on segregated education in Indianapolis. They demanded an educational system that separated students by race and required a fiery, charismatic spokesperson to articulate their demand. Along came D. C. Stephenson.[1]

David Curtis Stephenson (fig. 15.1) of Greenwood, Indiana, the grand dragon of the Klan, had an open invitation to the offices of Mayor John Duvall and Governor Ed Jackson to monitor the pulse of race relations in Indianapolis. Stephenson, a Texas-born door-to-door salesman, was a powerful political force in Indianapolis city government and was elected grand dragon not only of Indiana but also of twenty-two other northern states. He was a Prohibitionist and a fierce defender of white womanhood.

Predictably, Stephenson was also a fiery opponent of integrated education who fought fiercely to influence the Indianapolis Public School Board commissioners to adopt a resolution to construct a segregated African American high school. Like other governmental officials or community leaders who shared his racist and political doctrines, Stephenson considered African Americans to be racially and intellectually inferior and devoid of the basic standards of morality and civility. He envisioned "mixing of the races" of Black and white students as the first step in the destruction of white civilization.[2]

On March 15, 1925, Governor Ed Jackson introduced Stephenson to a young Irvington schoolteacher, Madge Augustine Oberholtzer. Oberholtzer was an educator and manager of the Indiana Young People's Reading Circle, a special section of the Indiana Department of Public Instruction. On January 12, 1925, she encountered Stephenson while attending Governor Jackson's inauguration party. They developed a relationship and met for dinner on several occasions. She served as Stephenson's aide during the 1925 session of the Indiana General Assembly. Later, she established herself in the highest echelons of state government to advocate for her reading programs, which faced termination because of budgetary constraints. Ultimately, Oberholtzer ended the relationship, and this development angered Stephenson considerably. He sought revenge.

Stephenson telephoned Oberholtzer and told her that he would ensure that her Reading Circle program received funding if she met him before he left on a trip to Chicago. His associates picked her up at her home and drove her to his mansion a few blocks away. She was attacked and was forced to consume a large quantity of alcohol before she was taken to the railroad station, where she was forced into Stephenson's private car. En route, he brutally raped her and cannibalized a portion of her body.[3]

Stephenson took Oberholtzer to Hammond, Indiana, and checked into a hotel, where he forced her to identify herself as his wife so that they could share a room. The next morning, she asked one of Stephenson's associates to drive her to a drugstore. There she purchased a bottle of mercuric chloride tablets, which she ingested in a suicide attempt. She was returned to Indianapolis, and on her deathbed, she signed a statement that detailed her horrid experience with Stephenson.[4]

On April 14, 1925, she died as the result of a staph infection from the bites and of kidney failure due to mercuric poisoning. On November 14, 1925, Stephenson was convicted of rape and second-degree murder and sentenced to life in prison. In the aftermath of this horrific event, the membership of the Ku Klux Klan dwindled, as many saw the hypocrisy of his campaign to protect white womanhood. This tragic event was a fitting testament to the hypocrisy of a man who championed the creation of a segregated Crispus Attucks High School, the denigration of the African American community, and the glorification of white supremacy.[5]

SIXTEEN

CRISPUS ATTUCKS HIGH SCHOOL

"Miracle in the Ghetto"

DURING THE 1920S, AFRICAN AMERICANS glanced backward into the late nineteenth century to gain a lucid perspective on education and to examine the history of great leaders in the field of education. They longed for an iconic figure in which they could invest their hopes for a system that would elevate their people and deliver them from the status of second-class citizenry. Perhaps they could glean wisdom from the leaders' philosophy and apply it to an Indianapolis educational system that would be specifically designed for struggling African Americans.

Majority citizens gained their educational inspiration from Greek philosophers or former presidents and statesmen whose biographies and photographs adorned their textbooks, but because many of those figures were former slave owners, this prospect was not considered in the African American community. Black Indianapolis longed for someone who could capture the spirit and determination of its people. Someone whose name was synonymous with excellence in education.

One such leader was Booker T. Washington, whose photograph proudly hung in classrooms in many of inner-city Black schools. Blacks were so proud of his leadership in America that Indianapolis Public School 17 was named in his honor. Many Black families proudly named their sons Booker T. African Americans realized that education was the key to the future, and who better to represent this ideal than Booker T. Washington?

Booker Taliaferro Washington was the great African American educator of the nineteenth and twentieth centuries and one of the most powerful and influential African Americans in the country. On July 4, 1881, he founded Tuskegee Institute, a segregated college for African American students in Tuskegee, Alabama. He served as an adviser to many US presidents and championed the advancement of African Americans through education and industry. He traveled throughout the country with his message that a quality education is a prerequisite to gaining acceptance and respect among majority Americans. His message was received favorably in Indianapolis, and many local educators were determined to stress the importance of education in the African American community. Many progressive families regarded education as a vehicle of empowerment and worked tirelessly to realize Washington's vision.[1]

According to the Indianapolis Public School System's records, in 1908, there were eighty Blacks enrolled in the system, and twelve years later the number skyrocketed to eight hundred. African American and white students attended class together, and there was no degree of racial separation in the classrooms.[2]

In the early 1920s, the social environment, greatly affected by the influx of African Americans, was ideal for a well-organized, racist campaign to justify the fears of the white populace. Enter David Curtis Stephenson and his racist campaign, which infiltrated municipal, state, and federal branches of Indiana government. From the Indiana State House to the municipal government to the Indianapolis Public Schools Board, many officials were either Ku Klux Klan members or sympathizers.

The racist doctrines espoused by the Ku Klux Klan in their nightly neighborhood meetings around the city motivated the white citizenry to take action. Many white residents feared that an integrated classroom would lead to intermarriage and integrated housing, so they launched a campaign to extricate African American students from the Indianapolis public schools' classrooms. Community organizations such as the White Peoples Protective League, Capitol Avenue Protective Association, Mapleton Civic Association, White Supremacy League, Chamber of Commerce, and Parent-Teacher Organizations all swung into action to counter the influx of African American students.

A movement initiated by city government had as its goal the creation of an all-Black, segregated high school. There was a hot debate in the African American community and press that this measure flew in the face of the fairness of American citizenship. Although the majority of the African American community rejected the school proposal, a few Black residents concurred. They believed that a segregated high school would provide employment for Black educators and create a more positive learning environment for African American youngsters.[3]

Dr. John Morton-Finney, the first educator hired by Principal Mathias Nolcox to teach at Crispus Attucks High School (who possessed five law degrees and eleven bachelor's degrees and spoke seven languages) commented on the opposition to the school in his memoirs: "I saw Attucks from the time they put the first spade in the ground until it was completed. When they were first talking about opening it, it was not very favorable with the black community. As a matter of fact, it was hostile. This was the situation then: In Indianapolis, the highest thing in the way of education that a black could aspire to was to be among the graduates of Shortridge High School—you didn't need anything else in the world—that was tops. If you graduated from Shortridge, you had everything."[4]

One opponent of the segregated high school was Archie Greathouse, a business owner and community activist who went door-to-door in his quest to scuttle the plans for the school. His daughter, Ruth, was a student at an integrated high school and was scheduled to graduate soon.[5]

The community debate continued, and several suits were filed and appealed, but ultimately the city government appropriated funds to build a segregated high school. Initially, they agreed to name the school Thomas Jefferson High School, after the third president, who was a slave owner. The African American community strongly opposed this action and agreed on the name Crispus Attucks, the first American killed in the American Revolutionary War.[6]

Crispus Attucks High School opened on September 12, 1927. It was constructed to accommodate 1,000 students, but surprisingly, 1,350 students appeared at the front door on the first day of school. According to Dr. Stanley Warren, a Crispus Attucks High School graduate, social studies teacher, and professor emeritus at DePauw University, "There were probably three or four hundred students who came, but were not expected so they just came out of the wood work."[7]

Mathias Nolcox (fig. 16.1), born in the African American settlement of Lyles Station in 1868, was appointed the first principal. Although Crispus Attucks High School was a magnificently constructed, expertly designed edifice, a great deal of the furniture, equipment, and educational material was of the lowest quality. Nolcox demanded that Crispus Attucks High School receive the same consideration afforded to white high schools. He recognized the level of apathy and lack of concern vis-à-vis the success of Crispus Attucks High School and immediately took action.

Nolcox searched the nation and recruited the finest and best-credentialed African American faculty available. Many of these educators obtained master's and doctoral degrees and were prohibited from employment at southern colleges and universities because of Jim Crow laws. In essence, college professors were recruited to teach high school students.

Nolcox—mindful of the fact that many members of the Indianapolis Public School Board considered Crispus Attucks to be merely a "colored high school" with no prospects of high academic achievement or quality education—created

Fig. 16.1 Mathias Nolcox, first principal of Crispus Attucks High School. Courtesy of Crispus Attucks Museum, Indianapolis Public Schools.

and nurtured an educational environment wherein educational excellence was the norm and not the exception. Teachers were encouraged to create a classroom environment that demanded dedication, perseverance, and hard work, with the prospects of a college education in the future. He demanded an educational institution that was superior to any other in the system, and this course of action angered the commissioners of the Indianapolis Public School Board.[8]

The school's expansive curriculum included advanced mathematics, foreign languages, music, social studies, and health education classes. During World War II, Blanche Crossen sponsored the Junior Red Cross in 1941 and spearheaded the growth of war support activities throughout the school. The program sent food, bandages, toilet kits, and pillowcases to the United Service Organization and veterans' hospitals, and during the Christmas season, its members sent Christmas trees to the troops, wrote letters, and sent gifts to students in war-torn areas.

Two years later, the curriculum expanded to include a civil service auto mechanics program that was a component of the War Production Training Program. Throughout the school, there were war bond and stamp sales and the collection of paper, metal, coat hangers, and Victrola records.[9]

Although the majority of the students were from impoverished backgrounds, college attendance was a distinct possibility for Crispus Attucks graduates. Many teachers pooled their personal financial resources and networked with college admissions departments, many of which were from historically Black colleges and universities. They made sure that their students reached the summit of their academic potential. Many of the early colleges and universities that educated Crispus Attucks students were the neighboring Central State and Wilberforce Universities of Ohio, Kentucky State University, and Tennessee State University.

A DECADE OF TURMOIL

Lockefield Gardens

THE GREAT MIGRATION WAS THE mass movement of approximately six million African Americans from the southern United States to urban centers in the Northeast, Midwest, and West. This mass movement occurred between 1916 and 1970. In Indianapolis, many migrants were former residents of Mississippi, Tennessee, and Kentucky, while migrants from other states relocated principally to Chicago, Detroit, and other cities in the North. This mass exodus from the South was precipitated by poor economic conditions, racial terrorism, political disenfranchisement, and lack of employment opportunities.

As they settled into their new urban environment, African Americans wanted to compare and contrast their existence in the North with their painful memories of the South. They considered many questions: Was our move to the North wise and justified? Will we be accepted as Americans by the majority population? What measures can we take to earn our place in society as respected and worthy citizens? Are we equipped to live harmoniously and survive in the North? Should we discard the horrible memories of the past, or should they empower us to face new challenges in the future? Can we gain strength and resolve from our Black counterparts in the South, mobilize our resources, and march toward freedom and equality?

Many of these migrants were cognizant of the Springfield, Illinois, race riot of 1908. From Black newspapers or word of mouth, news of this horrific event spread like wildfire in large metropolitan areas and in rural towns of the South. The riots were sparked by the alleged rape of two white women and the death of the father of one of the women. Immediately, two Black men purported to be involved in the crime were arrested and jailed. When news of the incident circulated, an angry crowd of white Americans stormed the jail to apprehend and possibly lynch the Black men. When the crowd discovered that the men had been transferred to another penal institution, they became further enraged. To exact revenge, they attacked African American neighborhoods, murdered its citizens in the streets, and destroyed many businesses. The state militia rushed to town to quell the riot and restore order.[1]

In 1917, the *Indianapolis Recorder* apprised its readers of racial strife in Springfield's neighbor East Saint Louis, Illinois, less than three hundred miles from Indianapolis. World War I was on the horizon, and many of the major industries were in need of laborers to compensate for the loss of white men who had marched off to war. Simultaneously, there were many newly arrived European immigrants competing for the jobs sought by African Americans, and racial problems resulted. Many of these immigrants were on the margins of American civil society and directed their anger toward African Americans. This anger was transported to the workplace where both groups were employed.

In various incidents of labor unrest, migrants blamed African Americans for taking jobs that they regarded as their own. This dispute led to an all-out racial war. As a result of the riots and vandalism, two hundred African Americans were killed, six thousand lost their homes, and the economy lost nearly $8 million.[2]

In the *Indianapolis Recorder*, newly arrived Black immigrants kept abreast of developments in the South, and they were outraged by these events but emboldened by the ways fellow African Americans dealt with them and gained power. Perhaps these factors could motivate them to be successful in the North. They were also empowered in their fight when they read newspaper articles of other peoples of color, even in distant lands, who struggled to be free of oppression. The triumphs of African Americans in sports or entertainment gave them great pride and further validated their existence in the North.

The soundtracks of Indiana Avenue during the 1930s and 1940s were exciting and colorful. They carried a mixture of reactions to several events that captured Indianapolis's and the world's attention. They featured soundbites of the footsteps of entertainment patrons bustling up and down its corridors as they admired entertainers in the hottest nightspots. The pounding of courtroom gavels by angry judges as they dispensed injustice to African Americans in sleepy backwater towns of the South. The rapid rifle fire and thunderous explosions of munitions on battlefields in faraway places with strange names like Addis Ababa, Asmara, or Agordat. The deafening roar of jubilant spectators in Munich, Germany, who watched sprinter Jesse Owens cross the finish line and dispel the myth of Adolf Hitler's "Aryan superiority." The crackles and static of tiny radios in houses full of Black folks in urban America listening to a commentator give a blow-by-blow account of a Joe Louis heavyweight championship fight. This was Indianapolis, and this was the 1930s and 1940s!

Then came coverage of the Scottsboro Boys, a case in which nine Black teenagers were charged with the rape of two white girls on a freight train traveling from Chattanooga to Memphis, Tennessee. On March 25, 1931, a group of Black and white teenagers hitched a ride on the train, and during the trip, the two groups of youngsters argued and ultimately fought. At the next stop, the white youths departed the train and informed local authorities that they had been set upon and beaten badly by the Black youngsters. Immediately, the authorities radioed ahead to stop the train and investigate the alleged attack. During the interrogation process, two white girls informed the authorities that they had been viciously raped and held captive by the Black youths. The youths were arrested, taken to trial, and ultimately imprisoned. After a series of court cases, one of the girls confessed that their story was false, and the charges were dropped and the Black youths released.[3] This story galvanized the Black community in Indianapolis and made them question their own social position: The July 31 edition of the *Indianapolis Recorder* headline read "4 Scottsboro Boys Escape Lynch Attempt." Could something that horrific happen here?

African Americans in Indianapolis daily covered current events in Africa and therein felt a certain amount of racial pride and power. They recognized their historical connection to the Black Continent and identified with their common struggles.

On October 3, 1935, Italy, under the command of dictator Benito Mussolini, invaded Ethiopia. Using the excuse of a border dispute between Ethiopia and the Somalian territory controlled by Italy and also the promotion of nationalism in response to the humiliating defeat at the Battle of Adowa, March 1, 1896, by Ethiopian forces, thousands of Italian soldiers entered Addis Ababa, Ethiopia's capital, on April 9, 1936. A beleaguered Emperor Haile Selassie went into exile in Jerusalem before the invading troops set foot in Addis Ababa. The League of Nations, an organization that was the prototype for the United Nations, condemned the invasion and imposed ineffective economic sanctions on Italy. The front page of the May 9, 1936, edition of the *Indianapolis Recorder* was emblazoned with the headline "Emperor Selassie, Royal Family Exile in Jerusalem."[4]

Many of the African American churches in Indianapolis were deeply concerned with this invasion because of Ethiopia's biblical connections; Emperor Selassie was purported to be a direct descendant of King Solomon and Empress Sheba of the Bible. Mussolini later allied himself with German dictator Adolf Hitler during World War II.

International events in the news gave Indianapolis African Americans the opportunity to see triumph in spite of racial bigotry and injustice. African Americans gained courage and perseverance in the struggle against racism, whether they were being refused admission in a downtown movie theater or being refused a handshake. In essence, international events gave Indianapolis African Americans the will to struggle toward freedom and societal acceptance.

An international sporting event gave Blacks in Indianapolis another reason to be proud. The Games of the XI Olympiad, the Summer Olympics, opened August 1, 1936, in Berlin, Germany, against a backdrop of international outrage—the world's reaction to German racism, discrimination, and, most importantly, antisemitism. The German leader and dictator Adolf Hitler, a proponent of Aryan racial superiority, wanted to declare to the world the legitimacy of his racist beliefs. Jesse Owens, a Black Ohio State University track star, shocked the world by winning four gold medals and thus dispelling Hitler's racist beliefs. The spectacle of Owens standing on the first-place victory pedestal above the heads of conquered German athletes so infuriated Hitler that he quickly departed the stadium without recognizing Owens's feats or shaking his hand.

In Indianapolis, Hitler's refusal to acknowledge and shake the hand of the victor, Jesse Owens, prompted the editor of the *Jewish Post* to pen a response illustrating that Hitler's edict of Aryan superiority did not challenge the integrity of some Germans in the crowd. He wrote: "In the German citizen's enthusiastic praise for Jesse Owens, Negro track marvel, may be gained an indication of the adherence of the Nazis to the tenets of the Hitler philosophy of Aryanism. Despite Hitler's ugly refusal to recognize Owens, which however, was to be expected, the spectators cheered the United States athlete unreservedly and acknowledged his super-human ability in no less a sincere demonstration of homage than as an American sports crowd would give at a similar performance."[5]

Interestingly, the politics and international intrigue generated by the Munich Olympics departed the track field and climbed into the boxing ring. Joe Louis Barrow, also known as the Brown Bomber, held the US Heavyweight Boxing Championship from 1937 until 1949. Many Indiana Avenue patrons, proud of his African American heritage, gathered around the radio in their homes, nightclubs, and various businesses to listen to his championship bouts. During this time, Adolf Hitler's antisemitic and Aryan superiority doctrines continued to circulate throughout Europe and the world.

In the ring, Louis reigned victorious over all opponents until he faced the German Max Schmeling on June 19, 1936, at Yankee Stadium, in New York. This bout shocked the world as the less talented Schmeling defeated Louis to capture the heavyweight crown. Schmeling's victory over an African American seemed to substantiate Hitler's claim of Aryan superiority. Humiliated, Louis vowed to regain his crown and spent a few years sharpening up his skills for a return match with Schmeling.

On June 22, 1938, the Louis/Schmeling bout returned to Yankee Stadium in front of a crowd of seventy thousand spectators and tens of millions of listeners around the world. Watching what was predicted to be a bruising, bloody rematch that would be decided in the final rounds, the crowd was shocked. The fight lasted two minutes and four seconds, and Louis battered Schmeling with a series of swift attacks, forcing him against the ropes and giving him a paralyzing body blow. Schmeling was knocked down three times and only managed to throw two punches in the entire bout. On the third knockdown, Schmeling's trainer threw in the towel.

Indianapolis that night was a scene of jubilation. Revelers drove up and down Indiana Avenue, and patrons danced in the streets. Some bars gave drinks on the house, and shouts of "Thank you, Jesus" and "Wow-Wee" were heard all around African American Indianapolis. On July 7, 1938, *Indianapolis Recorder* editorialist Pickens, who attended the championship bout, wrote:

> There were more cheers for Louis and some boos from Schmeling. Who can wonder: There were "racial minorities" in the vast throng, including many Jews who had come with prayers in their hearts that Hitler's man would go down in defeat and so humble the Aryan in a minute. But, they did not expect what happened. Nobody did, except perhaps Louis himself, and he was half wrong, for he said he would "stop that smellin'" in round two, while he actually stopped him in about the middle of round one. You see, they say it was two minutes and four seconds "of fighting" but it was not.[6]

Entertainers and patrons alike celebrated Joe Louis's victory as they paraded up and down Indiana Avenue with shouts of joy. Guitarist Bill Gaither recorded his most famous hit, "Champion Joe Louis," on the day of Louis's victory.

These great news stories of the 1930s demonstrated the results of decades of struggle throughout the country and around the world and motivated African Americans to demand better living conditions at home.

In the aftermath of the historic Louis/Schmeling rematch, a program developed to improve living conditions for African Americans in Indianapolis. Housing conditions in many African American communities were abysmal, and citizens looked to city government for a resolution to this terrible problem.

In retrospect, from the late nineteenth century until the third decade of the twentieth century, the territory surrounding the White River and Indiana Avenue comprised overgrown vegetation, large trees, and swampland. Many of the shacks and shanties constructed on the banks of the White River had outdoor toilets and water pumps. These dwellings were occupied by Native Americans, free African Americans, and former slaves before and after the Civil

Fig. 17.1 The Martin family, first residents of Lockefield Gardens. Courtesy of Leslie F. Martin.

War, primarily from Mississippi, Tennessee, and Kentucky. This land was located in the western sector of Indianapolis, and the settlement there predated its incorporation as a city. More than one hundred years later, this territory proved to be very important to African Americans and their rightful place in Indianapolis society.

During Franklin Delano Roosevelt's New Deal of the 1930s, in twenty states the Public Works Administration constructed fifty public housing projects formerly blighted areas primarily occupied by low-income Americans of color. In Indianapolis, the public housing project was named in honor of Erie Locke, a city councilman who represented this area in the 1860s and 1870s. It was designed by the Russ and Harrison Architecture Firm and constructed by the N. P. Severin Company of Chicago, and it comprised 24 buildings and 748 apartment units.[7]

Lockefield Gardens opened in 1938, and among the amenities were a central mall, four playgrounds, a school (William D. McCoy Public School 24), and a small commercial strip. Many Black veterans of World War I had previously inhabited "shotgun shanties" (shacks with a large room with only front and back doors), outdoor latrines called privies, and water pumps from the previous century. African American families felt empowered to relocate to housing with indoor heat and toilets, electricity, and water service. Many felt that their contribution of service in the war had been rewarded.

When it opened, Lockefield Gardens was racially segregated, but it offered low-income African Americans living accommodations to which they were not accustomed. The first family to establish residency in the Lockefield Gardens Public Housing Development were Reverend George Augustus Martin Sr. and Edith Williams Martin. They resided at 936 West North Street in the apartments. Reverend Martin was a highly esteemed traveling Baptist minister who conducted services in many churches in the city, state, and region, and his wife, Edith, raised the children in their home. They were photographed (fig. 17.1) in their living room, relaxing with their two sons, George Augustus Jr. and Leslie Frederick. Other children, born later, were Edith Lucille, John Frank, and Joseph Wendell Martin. Their daughter, Edith Lucille, was the first baby born in the Lockefield Gardens. The Martin family proudly presented a strong, cohesive, respectful family unit that served as a prototype for other families who would reside in the Lockefield Gardens.[8]

HEROES OF WORLD WAR II

AFRICAN AMERICANS HAVE PLAYED SIGNIFICANT roles in the defense of the United States. On March 5, 1770, Crispus Attucks, a citizen of African American and Native American (Wampanoag) descent, was killed in a skirmish with British soldiers during the Boston Tea Party demonstration. He was the first American killed in the Boston Massacre, which sparked the American Revolutionary War when Americans demonstrated against a government controlled by the British.

Almost two hundred years later, during the Civil War, the Twenty-Eighth US Colored Battalion, an all–African American troop, left Indianapolis en route to Washington, DC, where they were stationed in the city primarily to protect the capital. The Twenty-Eighth Regiment sustained heavy casualties in the Battle of the Crater at the Siege of Petersburg, Virginia, on July 30, 1864. Nearly half of the soldiers were killed or wounded.

Indianapolis is proud of the many men and women who gallantly served this great nation during its many wars. Many of them made outstanding contributions to the protection and welfare of our democracy but have not received their proper and just acknowledgment. Many believed that if they exhibited undying loyalty to the country and shed their blood on foreign soil, America would recognize their humanity and welcome them as brothers and sisters.

One such individual, who became one of the first teachers employed by Crispus Attucks High School, distinguished himself on the battlefield and, later, as a superb educator in the classroom. He became a role model of excellence that inspired many of his students to strive toward distinction in the classroom. During one of his classes, he exhorted his students: "You must remember, this is one thing that Negroes must get in their heads, many of them don't seem to understand this. . . . We didn't come here, we were brought here, we weren't brought

Fig. 18.1 John Morton-Finney, member of the World War I Buffalo Soldiers and a Crispus Attucks educator. Courtesy of Crispus Attucks Museum, Indianapolis Public Schools.

here to be put in college, we weren't brought here to become lawyers, doctors, college graduates, but to labor, and that's what they want us to do, to this day, in order to carry out that kind of system, segregated, separated, categorized." He later rejoiced when the sagacious advice that he preached in the classroom realized positive results in the African American community: "I could begin to see a change, and the change became great! They began to go to college, and colored people just didn't send their children to college! They became teachers, lawyers, doctors, dentists, architects. . . . I've seen tremendous change in the attitude of the colored people, here in the city."[1] During a White House ceremony in 1990, President George Herbert Walker Bush commented that "he told me that I was the second president that he's met, the first was Franklin Delano Roosevelt. But having met him I know that this is a risk to praise him, but I have to disagree with him. I hope you'll join me in commending a man who may be America's most seasoned scholar, John Morton-Finney."

John Morton-Finney (fig. 18.1) was born on June 25, 1889, to George Albert and Etta Gordon Morton-Finney in Union Town, Kentucky. His father was an ex-slave, and his mother was from a family of free African Americans. She died when he was fourteen, and his father sent him to live on his grandfather's farm in Nelson, Missouri. During his childhood, he learned about his ancestors who had migrated from Ethiopia to Nigeria before being captured and transported on ships to America during the period of slavery.

In 1911, Morton-Finney enlisted in the US Army, and he served in the Twenty-Fourth Infantry (Buffalo Soldiers Unit) during the conflict in the Philippines. He served with the American Expeditionary Force overseas in France as a sergeant of the 806th Pioneer Infantry in France and fought in the Meuse-Argonne Major Offensive in October 1918. During World War I, he received a citation from General John J. Pershing. He moved to Indianapolis in 1922 after his US Army discharge.

He held degrees from Lincoln University in Jefferson City, Missouri; Iowa State University in Ames, Iowa; Butler University in Indianapolis, Indiana; Abraham Lincoln College of Law; Springfield, Illinois; and the Indiana University School of Law in Indianapolis, and he studied seven languages: Latin, Greek, German, French, Spanish, Portuguese, and English. John Morton-Finney died, January 28, 1998, in Indianapolis.[2] Morton-Finney was among the first teachers hired at Crispus Attucks High School in 1927. This segregated high school was erected during the reign of David Curtis Stephenson and Ku Klux Klan sympathizers who aimed to separate public school students by race.

Harry William Brooks Jr. (fig. 18.2), future teacher of generals, was born on May 17, 1928, to Harry William Brooks Sr. and Nora Elaine Bailey Brooks. He

Fig. 18.2 Major General Harry Brooks. Courtesy of Crispus Attucks Museum, Indianapolis Public Schools.

attended public schools in Indianapolis and graduated from Crispus Attucks High School in 1947. He enlisted as a private in the US Army on May 21, 1947, at age nineteen and retired as a major general in 1976 after completing twenty-nine years of a successful military career.

Brooks graduated from Officer Training School in 1949 and received his Bachelor of Science degree from the University of Omaha in 1962 and a Master of Science degree from the University of Oklahoma in 1973. He attended the Army Command and General Staff College and the Army War College and completed the Stanford University Graduate School of Business Executive Program.

Highly decorated, Brooks became a major general in 1974, and during his military service, he received the Distinguished Service Medal, the Meritorious Service Medal, two Legion of Merit Medals, two Bronze Star Medals, and seven Air Medals. He was also recognized for his bravery by foreign governments. The Republic of Vietnam awarded him the Cross of Gallantry, and the Republic of Korea decorated him with the Cheon-Su Medal (Order of National Security Merit).

One of his most prominent mentees was General Colin Powell, who later became chairman of the Joint Chiefs of Staff and the US secretary of state. In the 2016 documentary about his alma mater, *Attucks: The School That Opened a City*, General Powell responded to the question of Brooks's influence on his military career. Powell replied, "Harry taught us how to be generals." Brooks's distinguished military career spanned nearly thirty years, and he retired in 1976. General Brooks died on August 27, 2017.[3]

General Benjamin Davis, the first African American US Army general, visited Crispus Attucks High School and made a lasting impression on students with his decorum, dignity, and distinguished military career. This event impressed one young student so profoundly that he set his goals to become a military officer. "I don't recall what he said, but I was fascinated with his appearance, his demeanor, and I just started to say, now that is what I want to do. . . . So that is where the seed was planted."[4] Norris Webster Overton was born to Owen Overton and Rosa Overton on January 6, 1926, in Clarksville, Tennessee. He graduated from Crispus Attucks High School in 1946 and five years later received his Bachelor of Science degree in accounting from Indiana University. He received his master's degree in business administration from the Air Force Institute of Technology in 1959 and graduated from the Advanced Management Program at Harvard University in 1972. Overton completed the Air Command Staff College and the Industrial College of the Armed Forces by correspondence and the Air War College by seminar.

In January 1963, General Overton assumed duties as the staff accounting and finance officer, Karamursel Common Defense Installation, Turkey. He was an associate professor of aerospace studies at the University of Iowa from 1964 to 1968, when he was reassigned as base comptroller, Tan Son Nhut Air Base, Republic of Vietnam. In 1969, he transferred to headquarters in the US Air Force, Washington, DC, as executive officer to the deputy assistant comptroller for accounting and finance.

In 1972, General Overton became the deputy chief of staff, comptroller, United States Air Force Academy, near Colorado Springs, Colorado. His military decorations and awards include the Legion of Merit with oak leaf cluster, Bronze Star Medal with oak leaf cluster, Air Force Commendation Medal, Air Force Outstanding Unit Award Ribbon, Republic of Korea Presidential Unit Citation, and the Republic of Vietnam Gallantry Cross with palm. General Overton was promoted to the grade brigadier general on May 1, 1979, with date of rank April 24, 1979.[5]

An October 30, 1925, United States War College Study document included the following statement in reference to African American military personnel: "He cannot control himself in the fear of danger to the extent the white man can. He is mentally inferior to the white man." Two decades later, a young Air Force pilot would refute this statement as he flew successful bombing missions in the air above Germany and distinguished himself during World War II. Charles Barkley Hall was born on August 25, 1920, to Frank Hall and Anna Barkley Hall in Brazil, Indiana. Hall was an all-star athlete who graduated from Brazil High School in 1938. He attended Eastern Illinois State Teachers College, where he ran track and played football while enrolled in the premedical program. During this time, a pilot training program was created in anticipation of the entry of the United States in World War II.

President Theodore Roosevelt established a training program for African Americans, the majority of whom were college graduates. They were sent to a training facility at Tuskegee Institute, Tuskegee, Alabama, a college founded in 1881 by African American educator and college president Booker T. Washington.

Hall was inducted into the US Air Corps on November 21, 1941, less than one month before the attack on Pearl Harbor. He was one of the first African American fighter pilots to participate in the training program, and he graduated on March 7, 1942. He joined the 99th Pursuit Fighter Squadron, which was a division of the 332nd Fighter Group.

In 1943, Hall became the first African American fighter pilot to destroy an enemy aircraft. The strike on the German aircraft occurred on July 2, 1943, while he was flying with the 99th Fighter Squadron. He was on an escort mission of

B-25 medium bombers on a raid on Castelvetrano in southwestern Sicily, Italy, when he shot down the Focke-Wulf FW 190 Wurger while in a P-40 aircraft.

He described this encounter: "It was my eighth mission and the first time I had seen the enemy close enough to shoot him. I saw two Focke-Wulfs following the bombers just after the bombs were dropped. I headed for the space between the fighters and bombers and managed to turn inside the Jerries [Germans]. I fired a long burst and saw my tracers penetrate the second aircraft. He was turning to the left, but suddenly fell off and headed straight into the ground. I followed him down and saw him crash. He raised a big cloud of dust."[6]

General Dwight David Eisenhower personally visited Hall at his base in Italy and congratulated him for his bravery and meritorious service in protecting aircraft with his Tuskegee Air Unit during World War II. Hall was awarded the Distinguished Flying Cross for his service in World War II. After the war, he remained in the service and retired from the air force with the rank of major. Charles Barkley Hall died November 22, 1971.[7]

On June 18, 2002, the Charles B. Hall Airpark in Oklahoma City was opened in honor of Major Hall. A memorial tribute read, "A Tuskegee Airman and highly decorated pilot from the 99th Pursuit Squadron, which was part of the 332nd Fighter Group. During World War II, Major Hall was the first African-American pilot to down an enemy aircraft in combat. He flew 198 combat missions over Africa, Italy and other parts of Europe and was the first African-American to receive the Distinguished Flying Cross."[8]

For these airmen, the act of flying was a symbol of liberation for themselves and all African Americans. As recounted by former First Lady Michelle Obama, one of those first pilots, a man named Charles DeBow, put it this way: "He said that a takeoff was, in his words, a never failing miracle, where all the bumps would smooth off, you're in the air, out of this world, free."[9]

Charles Henry DeBow Jr. (fig. 18.3) was born on February 13, 1918, to Charles Henry DeBow and Anna Sue DeBow in Indianapolis. He attended the Mary Elizabeth Cable School 4 and Crispus Attucks High School, where he was president of the student council in 1935 and graduated the following year. He attended Indiana University for two years with a premedical major and became disenchanted with the social atmosphere of the university. He transferred to the all–African American Hampton Institute in Hampton, Virginia, where he majored in business administration.

He was inducted into the US Army Air Corps on July 26, 1941, and enrolled in the flight training program before joining the all–African American Tuskegee Airmen of World War II. The February 27, 1982, edition of the *Indianapolis Recorder* reported:

Fig. 18.3 Lieutenant Colonel Charles DeBow. Courtesy of Crispus Attucks Museum, Indianapolis Public Schools.

He was a member of the first class of Negro cadets graduated from Tuskegee Army Air Field on March 7, 1942 and was commissioned as a pilot along with Benjamin D. Davis, Jr, Lemuel R. Curtis, George S. Roberts and Mac Ross. The 99th was deployed overseas to fight in the European Theater and after 52 missions aboard a P-51 Mustang, DeBow was injured and lost his flight status. When he returned home, after the war, the young lieutenant colonel married and continued his education and eventually worked as a high school teacher and university professor in Indiana. Before his 18 years of active and 4 years of reserve duty had ended, the pilot had served as commanding officer of the original 301st Fighter Squadron after first serving as an adjutant in the 100th Fighter Squadron with Lieutenant George Knox also of Indianapolis.[10]

The March 1942 edition of *Life* magazine published an article about the newly incorporated Tuskegee Airmen. It read in part: "White instructors of the 99th agree that their Negro charges, by virtue of exceptional eye sight, courage and coordination, will prove crack combat pilots. Upon their performance and promise hang the hope of additional thousands of aspiring Negro fliers throughout the land?"[11]

The February 2, 1970, edition of the *Indianapolis Recorder* featured an article that highlighted DeBow's position as supervisor of the Neighborhood Youth Corps. This program provided employment for low-income youth in public and parochial schools, community agencies, and federal, state, and municipal offices. Charles Henry DeBow Jr. died on April 4, 1986, in Indianapolis.

On the Crispus Attucks Tigers, former football players learned not only how to block and tackle their opponents on the field but how to be outstanding young men dedicated to community service. Graham Edward Martin coached for several decades, mentored young men and women, and changed their lives. He was a mild-mannered coach on the sidelines and an outstanding educator in the classroom.

Graham Edward Martin was born on January 18, 1917, in Tobacco Port, Tennessee, to Charlie Martin, a tobacco farmer, and Carrie Martin, a homemaker. He was the youngest of four children who moved to Indianapolis with their mother after the death of their father. In 1930, he temporarily resided in the Home for Friendless Colored Children with fifty other youngsters, whose ages ranged from two years to eighteen years. In spite of his humble beginnings, Martin was determined to succeed in life and exhibited this desire to overcome obstacles, persevere, and excel in the classroom.

In 1933, Martin entered Crispus Attucks High School, where he continued to excel in the classroom and was president of the class of 1937, French club, student council, and boxing club. He found time to distinguish himself on the football field and was a star player on the team coached by the legendary Alonzo Watford. In 1938, Martin entered Indiana University on an academic scholarship with a profound desire to major in his favorite subject, history. To purchase clothes and school supplies for his education at Indiana University, he earned extra money as a redcap, carrying passengers' luggage at the Greyhound station in downtown Indianapolis. His love of football continued, and he became a star lineman on the college team coached by Bo McMillin.

Martin vividly remembered working as a strike breaker at a plant in southern Indiana during his college days and living inside the plant during the entire summer. Union members lined up with picket signs outside the plant and shouted epithets at the strike breakers. Their demonstrations did not faze Martin because he was determined to earn money so that he could return to college and continue his education. Once he returned to campus, the first assignment in his English class required him to write a paper about any significant event he experienced during the previous year. Martin chose his experience at the plant and wrote a paper that was considered the best in the class. It was displayed on a billboard in the English Department for the entire semester.

In 1941, Martin graduated from Indiana University and received a Bachelor of Arts degree in history. According to his former teacher at Crispus Attucks, Andrew Ramsey, an Indiana University alumnus who taught foreign languages, because of Martin's outstanding academic record at Indiana University, he earned a Phi Beta Kappa honor, but he never received it because racial issues were raised by the nominating committee. Later, he received a fellowship to study at Howard University, and by 1942, he was completing his master's degree in history when he received his draft notice.

Martin recounted the event: "I told them I was as patriotic as anybody, and didn't in any way shun the armed forces, but since what little money I had was involved in the school, I wished they would let me finish my course. So they wrote me back in a very short time and said, 'You stay there and we'll contact you again.'"[12]

He was drafted by the army, but he recalled, "I considered the Army was too dirty for me, crawling in all that mud and stuff . . . I was supposed to report to an Army place there in Alexandria, Virginia . . . I think 6:00 o'clock in the morning. That kind of made me angry; that's too early in the morning. So I joined the Navy. I was supposed to report August, the first. I joined the Navy July 31st."[13]

In the navy, Martin was trained at the Great Lakes recruitment station, located north of Chicago, and stayed on as company subcommander to train other recruits until 1943. During his stay, he played football on the squad coached by Tony Hinkle, of Butler University fame. The team went 10–2 that year, beating Notre Dame 19 to 14. In 1944, he began officer training with sixteen other men of color under Robert Smalls; all sixteen finished the training, which was unheard of at the time. Martin said of the training, "I think most of us felt that this was leading to something. We knew that they weren't spending that much time for nothing, so we were hopeful that it would end up with our being officers."[14]

Only thirteen were commissioned as officers in March 1944. But lightning struck in the life of Graham Edward Martin. He became a member of the "Golden Thirteen," the first African American men selected as officers in the navy during World War II. He was commissioned as an ensign.

Martin reflected, "As for being commissioned as part of that historic first wave of World War II–era African-American Naval officers, I felt good about it, and I just wondered what the next step was going to be and how they were going to use us. . . . I knew that the Navy didn't know what to do with us. I could tell immediately."[15]

Martin served on bases in Illinois, San Francisco, Hawaii, Eniwetok in the Marshall Islands, and Washington, DC, until he left the navy in 1946. At that point, Martin achieved his lifelong goal and became a teacher. He taught one year at the Bluefield State College in Bluefield, West Virginia, before he returned to his roots and taught history and physical education at his alma mater, Crispus Attucks High School. He became the head football coach from 1947 to 1982. On his place in history, he proudly remembered, "The events surrounding our becoming officers were small steps, but they led to great things, including the integration of the armed services, so I feel pretty good about that." During the summer of 2011, the city of Indianapolis renamed the Fall Creek, Sixteenth Street Park in his honor. Lieutenant Junior Grade Graham Martin died March 13, 1990, in Indianapolis.[16]

On July 26, 1948, President Harry S. Truman signed the executive order establishing the President's Committee on Equality of Treatment and Opportunity in the Armed Services committing the government to integrating the segregated military. A young Crispus Attucks graduate, John Wesley Lee, who had risen through the ranks, would make Indianapolis so proud. John Wesley Lee was born on February 13, 1924, to John Lee Sr. and Emma Lee in Indianapolis. He joined the navy on June 30, 1942, during the heights of World War II, and after leaving boot camp, he was admitted to the V-12 Officer Candidate Program at DePaul University in Chicago, Illinois, and graduated from the program. During an interview in 1977, Lee recounted that his parents were not thrilled with his decision to embark on a military career and wanted him to join the family business, which was a vegetable truck and vegetable stand at the City Market in downtown Indianapolis. He was commissioned as an ensign by the regular navy and became the first African American officer to be commissioned in the integrated armed forces. He believed that other African American navy men could become officers and worked behind the scenes to move things in the right direction.

In addition to a stint in World War II, Lee also served in the Korean War and was an assistant navigator for the USS *Kearsarge*. Also, he sailed on the USS *Toledo* and the USS *Wright* for various war and support missions. In 1960, Lee became the commanding officer of the Oceanographic Detachment Two Division. The unit prepared ocean surveys for the deployment of the Polaris submarines. Before his retirement in 1966, he served on the North Atlantic Treaty Organization staff in Paris and left the navy with the rank of lieutenant commander. Lee died on September 17, 2009.[17]

The tremendous contributions that women made in the military have not received proper recognition. From the bivouac medical station to the battlefield, women were integral personnel during the wars of our nation. More than four hundred women, some disguised as men, served on the battlefields during the Civil War.[18] African American house slave Cathay Williams served under the alias William Cathay. She was the first Black woman to enlist and the only documented woman to serve in the United States Army, posing as a man during the American Indian Wars.[19] Many outstanding women were to follow.

Alberta Stanley-White (fig. 18.4) was born on October 20, 1917, to Luke and Donie Stanley in Albany, Georgia. In 1937, she graduated from Crispus Attucks High School, and during her tenure there, she was employed as a domestic worker who earned fifty cents a week and dutifully gave her mother half of this amount to maintain their household.

In 1944, she received her practical nursing degree from the Chicago School of Nursing, and she joined the Women's Army Corps on July 27, 1945, in Indianapolis. She was sent to Fort Des Moines Army Base, Des Moines, Iowa, to train as a clerk. While on active duty, Stanley took a business course, became a clerk, and was assigned to the Fort Custer Hospital, near Battle Creek, Michigan. There, she assisted patients who survived war wounds. Then she was assigned to Gardiner Hospital, Chicago, where her primary responsibilities were assisting in the pediatric ward and working with young mothers. She fondly remembered attending an army-navy football game and watching fellow 1937 fellow graduate and class president Graham Martin play.

She was discharged from the army because of a reduction in force order and joined the Ready Reserve Duty. Assigned to Butler University, she became a black reservist. She carried similar responsibilities as when she was on active duty.[20]

She reflected, "The military impacted my life considerably. I got to meet people from all over the world. As patients, I would hear their life stories, sit with them when near death, find a priest or minister if they wanted and even prayed

Fig. 18.4 Alberta Stanley-White, member of the Women's Army Corps during World War II. Courtesy of Alberta Stanley.

with those who wanted prayer. Yes, I'd do it again! I had black and white friends. I have kept in touch with many of them through the years . . . I've received some obituaries."[21]

In 1940, as the United States prepared to enter World War II, millions of jobs were created in the defense industry, and African Americans who sought employment in this industry were subjected to discrimination and violence. African American labor leader A. Philip Randolph, president of the Brotherhood of Sleeping Car Porters, met with President Franklin Delano Roosevelt and demanded that he take action to address this problem. Roosevelt issued Executive Order 8802, which barred government agencies and federal contractors from refusing employment in industries engaged in defense production on the basis of race, creed, and color or national origin. The order required that the armed services, including the Marine Corps, recruit and enlist African Americans.[22]

On June 1, 1942, recruitment of the Montford Marines commenced. Thousands of African American men answered the call to defend their country and rushed to recruitment offices throughout the United States to join the war. The first recruits received basic training at the segregated Camp Montford Point in Jacksonville, North Carolina. Lancaster Price was among the first contingent of African American marines to vow to give their lives in defense of their country.[23]

Lancaster (Lanny) Warren Price was born on March 9, 1924, to John Morgan Price and Pearl Venetta Fields Price in the tiny coal-mining town of Montgomery, West Virginia. He was the youngest of three boys. His father was a coal miner, and his mother, a homemaker, was the major musical influence in his early years. She was reportedly an excellent vocalist at the small church attended by the family. He was inducted into the US Marine Corps in October 1944. Price was a member of the all-black Montford Point Marines, a group that was stationed in the South Pacific during World War II. As a member of the Special Service Marine Band, he entertained troops throughout the islands. He was honorably discharged in 1946 and came to Indianapolis to further his education. Lancaster Warren Price died on November 19, 2019.[24]

NINETEEN

THE 1950s

THE EARLY 1950S HERALDED AN age of renewed optimism for African Americans in Indianapolis as the impossible became possible. Ray Province Crowe (fig. 19.1), a young coach from the aptly named Whiteland, Indiana, took the Attucks High School basketball team to the pinnacle of success with two state championships in 1955 and 1956. It was the first time that an all-Black team, on any level in any sport, won a state championship in an integrated tournament.

The team (fig. 19.2) was led by Oscar Robertson (fig. 19.3), University of Cincinnati three-time All-American, 1960 Olympic gold medalist, and twelve-time National Basketball Association All-Star and Most Valuable Player, and members included Willie Merriweather, Bill Hampton, Bill Scott, Bill Brown, Shedrick Mitchell, John Gipson, Sam Milton, John Clemmons, Willie Burnley, and Johnny Mack Brown. They became legendary symbols of triumph over adversity. They were heroes not only on the basketball court but in many homes and classrooms across the city.

Beneath the celebration and excitement generated by these historic events, there was an undercurrent of racism, skepticism, anger, and resentment. Before the championship game of 1955, Crispus Attucks principal Russell Lane was summoned to the office of the superintendent of the Indianapolis Public School System. He may have anticipated a joyful meeting to congratulate him for the exemplary comportment of his players and other students during the basketball tournament. But this was not the case.

As he entered the room, he noticed the stern and troubled looks on the faces of the white men assembled. In attendance were the mayor, the superintendent, the chiefs of police and fire departments, and businessmen from downtown establishments. As he sat there perplexed, the following address was delivered: "Mr. Lane, it looks like your team's going to win the championship next Saturday

Fig. 19.1 Ray Provence Crowe, coach of the Crispus Attucks basketball teams of the 1950s. Courtesy of Indiana Historical Society.

Fig. 19.2 The 1955 Crispus Attucks state basketball champions. Courtesy of Indiana Historical Society.

night, the merchants downtown are frightened, after you win that championship colored people will come downtown and tear up the downtown, break out the windows, knock out the street lights and all that."[1] Principal Lane was informed that if Attucks won the championship, then the traditional celebratory event on the Monument Circle enjoyed by previous state championship victors would not take place. Instead, there would be a lap around the circle and then a trip to the Northwestern Park, located in the African American community.[2]

On March 19, 1955, the Crispus Attucks Tigers shook the world, defeating Gary Roosevelt High School 97 to 74. Oscar Robertson scored thirty points, and Wilson Jake Eison, future Indiana Mr. Basketball, scored thirty-one. After the game, the festivities began. The team departed the Butler Fieldhouse, traveled down Indiana Avenue in front of hundreds of jubilant fans, and arrived at the most historically significant, cherished monument in the city. They mounted the Indianapolis Fire Department's trucks, as was customary during the victor's celebration, took a few laps around the Monument Circle, and were whisked off to the Northwestern Park, deep in the African American community. They were honored at a bonfire that lasted an hour and then returned home. The

Fig. 19.3 Oscar Robertson. Courtesy of Indiana Historical Society.

time-honored festivities traditionally reserved for the winning state basketball
champions eluded the Crispus Attucks Tigers.[3]

During the 1950s, there were other sporting events that caught the eye of
Indianapolis residents in search of fun and amusement—for instance, baseball. America's fascination with baseball dates back more than a century, to

when trouser-clad white men played a baseball-like game with a wooden bat and round, soft ball, governed by their own momentarily revised rules. The earliest mention of baseball in the United States appears in a 1791 Pittsfield, Massachusetts, city ordinance that banned the playing of baseball within eighty yards of the town meeting hall.[4]

Throughout the decades, baseball became increasingly popular and achieved celebrity status as America's favorite pastime. During the early twentieth century, African Americans enjoyed baseball played on dusty fields in southern towns or neighborhood parks in major cities, but because of the racial climate of the day, teams were not permitted to engage in integrated league competition.

The Indianapolis Clowns were a professional baseball team established in the Tampa, Florida, area in the 1940s. The year-round warm temperatures accentuated with plenty of sunshine and beautiful palm trees provided the alluring environment in which Negro baseball developed. Many of the local male athletes played baseball throughout the year and therefore enjoyed an advantage over their athletic counterparts who resided in the cold-weather cities of the North.

Syd Pollock, a Tarrytown, New York, resident, organized the Indianapolis Clowns and originally named them the Ethiopian Clowns. Some members of the Negro League, established by Rube Foster and C. I. Taylor in 1920, with eight teams, considered the name Clowns to be disrespectful and stereotypically racist. They wanted to emphasize the fact that they were a legitimate baseball team worthy of the respect and admiration of other teams in the major leagues. Later, they were compelled to change their name to the Cincinnati Clowns and subsequently to the Indianapolis Clowns. Although they bore those cities' names, their main office was in Tarrytown, New York.[5]

As the team traveled from stadium to stadium across the country, neighborhood youngsters met them at the stadium door and asked if they could be batboys during the game. In Indianapolis, one enterprising and strategic-thinking youngster, Clifford Robinson, located the hotel that lodged the Clowns, went there, asked to be the batboy, and was given the job.[6]

Robinson served as the Indianapolis Clowns' batboy from 1946 to 1948. He got parental permission to travel with the team and considered the opportunity "a dream come true." He vividly and comically remembered many of the routines that kept the fans bursting with laughter during the games. Many of the most popular comedic routines involved Reece "Goose" Tatum, who later gained international fame with the Harlem Globetrotters basketball team; Ralph Bell, whose stage name was Spec Bebop, a little person from Daytona Beach who stood barely over three feet; and Richard King, whose stage name was King Tut.[7]

One comedy routine fondly remembered by Robinson featured Goose Tatum and King Tut, who sat on the infield grass with Tut in front. With two sets of bats as oars, they cut through imaginary waters to their fishing spot and rested their bats on the bottom of their invisible boat. Peacefully, each picked up a bat as a pole, cast an imaginary line, and fished. As they waited for a bite, Tut pointed up to the beauty of the day, and as he scanned the skies, he suddenly flinched, snapped one eye shut, and angrily wiped his face. He shook his fist at an imaginary bird, a portent of worse things to come. Then, the unexpected: Tut hooked a monster fish, with Goose a clinging appendage to his back. He quaked and shook from front to back and side to side with the ebb and flow of the huge invisible beast. His fishing pole flicked and seemed to bend, until the creature pulled the boat under and threw Tut and Goose separate ways in the menacing currents.

As they swam for their lives across the infield toward shore, and as their strokes brought their heads above water, each spat an impossible number of streams high in the air, seemingly from reservoirs unknown to even gluttonous camels.

Tut swam ashore, exhausted and almost drowned, near the pitcher's mound, and as he came to, gathered his strength, and arose, he noticed Goose prone, unmoving, heaped on the shore several feet away. A stethoscope pulled from a pocket affirmed life, but the joy of Tut's face again clouded as he pulled off his baseball cap, scratched his head, and risked a look upward as if to request divine assistance to restore consciousness to his tall companion.

First, he sat on Goose's waist and pumped his chest, and was doused anew with each thrust as a still comatose Goose sprayed him from some improbable source of water in his mouth. The crowd exploded with laughter.[8]

Although there was merriment during the game and comedic performances, other aspects of the team's travel were not as pleasant. While visiting major league stadiums throughout the country, the Indianapolis Clowns could not find accommodations in downtown hotels and restaurants and had to rely on the Green Book, which listed hotels and restaurants throughout the country that would accommodate African Americans. Many players lodged in African American hotels or private homes.[9]

Before each game at the major stadiums, the Indianapolis Clowns and other African American teams were denied entrance to the home team's dressing room and dressed in the visitors' dressing room or on their buses. The major league white players denied them the use of their facilities.[10]

During the early 1950s, the Indianapolis Clowns played at Victory Field and afterward headed to Indiana Avenue. Many of them were still in uniform, and

Fig. 19.4 Advertisement for the Indianapolis Clowns baseball team. Archives of Clifford Robinson.

they were greeted by admiring fans. Indianapolis was proud of the Indianapolis Clowns, and the Clowns appreciated the warm, wholesome welcome they always received. They played in stadiums from New York to Kansas City and from Michigan to Mississippi, and adoring fans waited in long lines to see the Clowns perform.

Young Robinson was paid a dollar a day for meals, and when he left the team in 1948, the team collected donations and bought him a brand-new Roadmaster bicycle with knee action, a rear luggage carrier that supported saddlebags, and fancy taillights. According to Robinson, "I was the pride of my Lockefield Gardens neighborhood and I considered myself the luckiest guy alive!"[11]

Although the Indianapolis Clowns were subjected to various forms of discrimination on the road, they persevered, disregarding a certain degree of slights. They were determined to make the baseball fans of African Americans proud. They were well aware of the racial climate in America and the problems that they might encounter, but this did not deter them from entertaining throngs of cheering jubilant fans wherever they appeared.

TWENTY

—ↄ∞—

THE ENTERTAINMENT INDUSTRY
FLEXES ITS MUSCLE

THE SOCIAL ATMOSPHERE OF THE fifth and sixth decades of the twentieth century in the Indianapolis African American community and entertainment industry reflected events occurring throughout America on a daily basis. The nation was in a whirlwind of turmoil. Civil rights protestors determined to change the course of American history conducted campaigns of civil disobedience and civil resistance. These events reported on television, on radio, in newspapers, and in other media sources became a daily staple for the news-consuming general public. Marches, boycotts, mass demonstrations, lunch-counter sit-ins, and other forms of protest were employed to gain national and worldwide coverage. Names like Dr. Martin Luther King Jr., Rosa Parks, and Malcolm X became symbols of struggle and resistance in the daily African American lexicon.

Indianapolis civil rights organizations such as the National Association for the Advancement of Colored People (NAACP) and the Urban League were at the forefront in the battle to preserve the gains made in the Black community thus far. Community leaders believed that the next frontier in the fight for freedom and equality was the entertainment industry.[1] Both civil rights organizations pondered questions facing the Black community: How can we battle discrimination in one of the most popular and powerful industries in Indianapolis? What strategies and mechanisms should we employ to fight discrimination in the lucrative entertainment industry? If we do not succeed, will this struggle have an adverse effect on Indianapolis entertainers of all genres? Could we destroy their careers? How could this battle affect the core of the city since the economic vitality of Indiana Avenue depended on the entertainment empire? Are we cutting off our nose to spite our face?

These questions were also important to other cities with large African American populations. Fortunately, the crowning achievements of this era of protests were the Civil Rights Act of 1964, the Voting Rights Act of 1965, and the Fair Housing Act of 1968. In the wake of these milestones in history came waves of inner-city riots in African American communities, in which protestors died and business districts burned, from 1964 through 1970.

In Indianapolis, African Americans struggled with issues of racial inequality in many spheres of the community, including the entertainment industry. Although, there were antidiscrimination laws designed to protect African Americans from overt racism, in many instances enforcement was negligible and clever business owners sought ways to circumvent these dictates.

From the onset of the twentieth century, there had been a history of systematic racial discrimination in the entertainment industry. Many establishments were segregated. One of the most glaringly obvious examples of virulent racism was the Riverside Amusement Park. It opened its doors at the beginning of the twentieth century in 1903. Although it was equipped with Ferris wheels, carousels, mechanical horses, and pantaloons-clad jugglers, other aspects of its operation were also visible to the general public: racism and discrimination. The amusement park had rigid segregation rules that prohibited African Americans from entering in any capacity other than custodial services.[2] Signs posted at the entrance read "Dogs and Negroes not Allowed." For decades this was the park's standard operating procedure, and some patrons basked in its exclusivity. An editorial titled "Riverside Hate Signs" appearing in the April 21, 1954, edition of the *Indianapolis Recorder* responded to the racist intent of these signs: "These signs, which takes you right back to the Ku Klux Klan days, read: 'Patronizing Whites Only Solicited.'"

But as gate receipts dwindled in the middle of the century, the park employed a new business model. The Polk's Milk Company, which was highly regarded in the African American community for its fair employment practices and economic support, stepped up to the plate. It convinced the administrators of the amusement park to allow African Americans the opportunity to enjoy the park on a limited basis. The plan, which involved a promotional campaign, allowed African Americans to enter the park and enjoy the entertainment one day per year. It stipulated that each patron must present a specified quantity of milk bottle caps for proof of patronage to the milk company. In 1963, after years of rigid discrimination, the local NAACP demonstrated against this racist policy, and the administrators relented and extended admission to African Americans.[3]

The Turf Club was a popular entertainment venue located on 16th Street and Lafayette Road, in close proximity to Indiana Avenue. Although it regularly featured the African American jazz genre, its patrons were exclusively white. Blacks could perform on stage or work in the kitchen, but they could not sit in the audience. A popular, white-owned night club located approximately a mile east of the Turf Club on Meridian Street also featured popular and jazz artists who were nationally or regionally known. In the early 1960s, it contracted jazz vocalist Flo Garvin.

In 1951, Garvin thrilled Indianapolis television viewers by becoming the first local African American entertainer to appear on the WFBM, channel 6, music program *Sentimental Journey*. She was backed instrumentally by the young guitarist Wes Montgomery, fender bassist Monk Montgomery, and drummer Sonny Johnson. She gained a substantial television fan base and was the first African American contracted to perform at the Embers, a plush, segregated nightclub on the Meridian Street entertainment strip. Before her first engagement, she was apprised of the rules and code of conduct. According to Garvin, "I was informed that during the intermission period between each set, I was required to go to the kitchen and sit quietly in a chair until I heard the band warming up for the next set."[4] The owner explained to her that social mingling and chatter with the high-class audience would be socially inappropriate and that some patrons might take offense. She listened to the directives but disobeyed them. "I refused and my contract was terminated." Decades later she mused, "I was very happy to have signed and contract and perform there with all the glitz, glitter and glamour, but racism got in the way."[5]

In the commercial district of downtown Indianapolis, similar practices existed. Although Indianapolis began to receive international recognition for its jazz entertainment greats, an undercurrent of racism continued to lurk beneath the surface. On March 12, 1960, Ron Woods, columnist of the *Indianapolis Recorder*, penned an article that detailed two racial discrimination incidents that occurred at the Turf Club. The Turf Club featured up-and-coming jazz artists and was very popular in the jazz community. The African American Wes Montgomery Trio, which featured guitarist Wes Montgomery, pianist and vibraphonist Buddy Montgomery, and bassist Monk Montgomery, performed there nightly.

A group of prominent Indianapolis residents, Gilbert Johnson, Laura Mays, Anthony Martin, and Dannis Harris telephoned the establishment and were granted reservations for a future performance. After arriving and being seated, they were approached by the owner, Mildred Thompson, and informed that there had been a clerical error and that there was no record of their reservations. Thompson demanded that the group immediately leave the establishment, and when they refused, she offered to seat them in a room in the basement. They refused and then departed.

Earlier that day a similar incident had occurred when John Torian, Patti Cox, Thomas Eubanks, and Michael Smith tried to gain entry into the establishment.

They too were refused service and asked to leave the premises. When the group refused, the owner informed them that "every business has the right to refuse service to whoever it wants. . . . We'd prefer not to serve Negroes here. . . . It's bad for the business."[6]

The group took the case to the Marion County Prosecutor's Office and was informed that an investigation would be conducted. After much delay, the prosecutor's office filed charges against Thompson, and she was arrested for violation of the Indiana Antidiscrimination Law and was released the same day. In spite of her legal battles with the city, Thompson displayed her undying loyalty to racism and bigotry, unfurling the Confederate flag and proudly flying it on the front lawn of her establishment for many months.

A decade later, another incident concerning the civil rights movement made activists even more determined to counter racism and strive toward freedom.[7]

In the early 1960s, Jimi Hendrix, the left-handed rock guitarist who years later made history at the legendary Woodstock Music Festival and became internationally famous with his signature song "Purple Haze," came to Indianapolis. Both he and his bandmate drummer, Billy Cox, were stationed in the US Army base in Fort Campbell, Kentucky. They traveled to Indianapolis for an engagement at the Brass Rail nightclub in the downtown entertainment district. They made contractual arrangements by telephone, but when they arrived at the venue, their reception surprised and disappointed them.

The owner had not realized that they were African American musicians, because of their northwest accents, and canceled their contracts on the basis of the club's policy of segregation. They were advised to return to Fort Campbell, Kentucky. Dejected and penniless, they ventured on to Indiana Avenue and entered a "battle of the bands" contest at the George's Bar nightclub so that they might earn gasoline money and return to their army base.

Their performance "brought down the house," and they assumed that they had won first place, but a superbly talented band called Baby Leon and the Presidents from Louisville, Kentucky, received a more thunderous applause and won the contest. Although Hendrix and Cox were defeated, the experience cemented their determination to take their artistry to the next level, and they headed to their next gig in Clarksville, Tennessee.[8]

In the downtown Indianapolis commercial establishments, African Americans were the recipients of racial discrimination and bigotry. In many of the department stores, African Americans were not allowed to try on shoes, hats, or other clothing items if they did not intend to purchase them immediately. Salespeople informed them that Caucasian patrons were concerned about a possibility of interpersonal contamination. They theorized that diseases harbored by

African Americans could be transmitted to Caucasian shoppers and adversely affect their stores' economic profile.

The tearoom of the L. S. Ayres department store did not welcome African American patrons but gladly employed them in the kitchen as cooks or waiters. Many former employees recounted the tearoom's stuffy, pretentious atmosphere wherein white women of high society, attired in gaudy hats with nets, white gloves that extended to their elbows, and pungent flowery perfume, were waited on "hand and foot" by hurrying African American waiters. In spite of the many indignities suffered by African Americans downtown, the Indiana Avenue entertainment industry served as a refuge where African Americans were served and entertained regardless of their race.[9]

Although during this period African Americans faced exhausting struggles for racial justice, equal rights, and fair employment practices, there were reasons for celebration, as Indiana Avenue and other African American neighborhoods experienced a renaissance of the arts and culture. This glitzy, glamorous entertainment boulevard continued to provide patrons with world-class entertainment throughout the year, and public demand called for additional entertainment venues. During these decades, there was an explosion of first-class entertainment venues, of which Indiana Avenue patrons were extremely proud. The *Indianapolis Recorder* announced the arrival of new and exciting entertainment nightspots, such as Sug's Sugar Bowl Tavern, the New and Swank Huddle Lounge, the Place to Play, the Blue Eagle Tavern, Al's British Lounge, and Scotty's Lounge. The determined warriors of Indianapolis had made great strides toward freedom![10]

THE BLACK COMMUNITY
BATTLES NEGATIVE STEREOTYPES AND
INTRODUCES JAZZ AND POETRY

THE ADVENT OF TELEVISION WAS an epic event and defining moment in the African American community in Indianapolis, especially in the heart of the city, Indiana Avenue. It also served as a barometer to gauge progress made by Blacks from previous decades. In the early 1950s, there were three television stations, whose programming was geared primarily toward the majority community. The television stations were WFBM, channel six, which hit the airways on May 30, 1949; WTTV, channel four, November 11, 1949; and WISH, channel eight, July 1, 1954.[1] The first and most popular television program to purportedly cause American viewers to buy millions of television sets was Milton Berle's *Texaco Star Theatre*, in 1948. This show was followed by the *Arthur Godfrey and His Friends Show* of 1949 and the *Ted Mack Family Hour* of 1951. The format of these extremely popular shows was based on slapstick comedy as presented by Milton Berle and music and guest interviews presented by Godfrey and Mack.[2]

There were only a few programs that featured topics, themes, or entertainment that generated interest in the African American community. These programs included the *Amos 'n' Andy Show*, the *Beulah Show*, and the *Stu Erwin Show*, all of which cast Blacks in a negative and comical light, portraying them as inarticulate, dull-witted buffoons who were subservient to the point of complete docility. From the conniving character of George "King Fish" Stevens of the *Amos 'n' Andy Show* to the childish, obedient, and blindly loyal maid Beulah in the *Beulah Show* to the slow-talking, bug-eyed character of Willie Best in the *Stu Erwin Show*, Blacks were portrayed as the minstrel characters of the previous century. The *Amos 'n' Andy Show* so infuriated certain segments of the Black community that its network, the Columbia Broadcasting System (CBS), was pressured by the National Association for the Advancement of Colored People (NAACP) to cancel the series in 1953.[3]

In light of the achievements and sacrifices made during the twentieth century, African Americans wondered whether this was their reward. How could they combat these negative stereotypes and march toward freedom and acceptance in the Indianapolis community? The movers and shakers of the civil rights community knew that these questions had to be addressed immediately.

Another aspect of the media that infuriated some segments of the Black community and jazz aficionados was the question of the genesis of jazz. Many jazz historians, scholars, and researchers constantly referred to New Orleans as the sole birthplace of jazz. Often they cited trumpeters Buddy Boden and Louis Armstrong, cornetist King Oliver, and pianist Jelly Roll Morton as the sole creators of jazz. Many books and magazine articles promoted this narrative without in-depth historical investigation. Local jazz entertainers took issue with this assessment and countered with the jazz luminaries from Indianapolis. The Crispus Attucks Music Department and the McArthur Conservatory of Music produced many outstanding entertainment artists of various genres, and this factor was ignored. The response to this slight led to the introduction of many notable jazz and rhythm and blues performers and poets.[4]

In weekly editions of the *Indianapolis Recorder*, there were articles that celebrated the jazz and rhythm and blues personalities who appeared primarily in the clubs on Indiana Avenue. Then, a historic breakthrough occurred. In 1951, John Lesley "Wes" Montgomery arrived on the scene. The introduction of Wes Montgomery to the world of jazz gave a new dimension to the musical impact and acceptance of the guitar. The piano, saxophone, bass, clarinet, and drums were considered legitimate jazz instruments, but when Wes Montgomery, influenced by jazz guitarist extraordinaire Charlie Christian, arrived on the scene jazz critics changed their opinions. Jazz aficionados realized that Wes Montgomery expanded the horizon of jazz and took it to a higher orbit in another direction.[5]

Montgomery's international notoriety and honors gave legitimacy to the jazz scene of Indianapolis and thereby empowered the Indianapolis African American community. His exposure in many of the jazz magazines and polls, including the highly influential *Downbeat* magazine, gave credibility to the Indianapolis jazz scene. He developed a style of playing that embellished the idiom of the jazz guitar and made it an instrument that generated electricity and excitement on the bandstand. Montgomery was an important factor in the empowerment of Indianapolis jazz during this decade. In spite of the negative stereotypes of African Americans presented in the media earlier in the mid-twentieth century,

Montgomery set the record straight and ushered in a period of sophistication and respect in the world of entertainment.

Montgomery was born on March 6, 1923, to Tom Montgomery and Frances Arrington Montgomery. He carried the moniker Wes throughout his life. Although Montgomery attended Crispus Attucks High School and was exposed to arguably the best music department in the Indianapolis Public School System, he did not have any formal music training. This factor rendered him unable to read chord symbols or notations throughout his musical career.

When Montgomery was nineteen, his appreciation of music took a "turn for the best" as he, by chance, heard the recording "Solo Flight" by the great jazz guitarist Charlie Christian. Of that life-changing experience, Montgomery commented, "When I heard Charlie Christian, I didn't know what to think because I hadn't heard anything like that. I hadn't even heard French guitarist Django Reinhardt yet. Christian got me all messed up."[6] In an April 1995 *Downbeat* interview with jazz critic Ralph J. Gleason, Montgomery said, "I got interested in playing the guitar because of Charlie Christian, like all other guitar player. There's no way out. I never saw him in my life, but he said so much on the records that I don't care what instrument a cat played, if he didn't understand and didn't feel and really didn't get with the things that Charlie Christian was doing, he was a pretty poor musician—[Charlie] was so far ahead."

Then lightning struck for Montgomery. On September 7, 1959, he hustled into Jacque Durham's Missile Room to perform a set. Jazz saxophonist Julian "Cannonball" Adderley was in town for a concert and dropped by to hear Montgomery perform. Duncan Schiedt, a music historian, attended the show and remembered the incident: "The set began and before the number was halfway through, Cannonball moved to a table directly in front of Montgomery who was already showing his marvelous unique technique. The next memory I have is that Cannonball leaned way back in his chair, kind of slumped and rolled his eyes to the ceiling as if 'knocked out,' which he evidently was. He stayed rooted to his table all the time I was there."[7]

The following morning, Cannonball telephoned Riverside Records producer Orrin Keepnews, who immediately signed Montgomery to a recording contract. Montgomery packed his bags for New York, where he recorded his first album as a leader, titled *A Dynamic New Sound: The Wes Montgomery Trio*. His new recording contract propelled him to national celebrity status. Although the album received mixed reviews, it paved the way for his next album, *The Incredible Jazz Guitar of Wes Montgomery*, which received rave reviews and is considered one of his best works of art. As a result of the tremendous popularity of this album, he received the *Downbeat* magazine's New Star Award in 1960.

From that point onward, his popularity skyrocketed, and jazz aficionados around the world asked, "Who is this Wes Montgomery from some place called Naptown?"

In 1965, Montgomery was nominated for two Grammy Awards for the album *Bumpin'*, and he received the Grammy Award for best instrumental jazz performance for "Goin' Out of My Head" in 1966. He was nominated for Grammy Awards again in 1968 for "Eleanor Rigby," and *Down Here on the Ground* and was nominated for *Willow Weep for Me*. In addition, he won *Downbeat* magazine's Critics Poll Award for best jazz guitarist in 1960, 1961, 1962, 1963, 1966, and 1967. Other jazz guitarists considered Wes Montgomery the greatest living jazz guitarist in the world. Sadly, he died of a heart attack at age forty-five on June 15, 1968, in Indianapolis.

Athletics and music were two activities that were popular in high schools in Indianapolis and received a great deal of exposure and student recognition. One student excelled in both arenas and was extremely popular on campus. He was an outstanding track and cross country star as well as a promising jazz student. He had to choose between the cinders of the track field or the chair in the practice sessions in the band room. The chair was victorious. Frederick Dewayne Hubbard was born on April 7, 1938, in Indianapolis to Earmon Hubbard Sr. and Delphia Hubbard. He received his early music training under the tutelage of John H. White, a music instructor at Arsenal Technical High School. Early in Hubbard's musical training, White did not permit him to play the trumpet because the instructor did not approve of his fingering technique. White insisted that Hubbard begin his musical training on the French horn. Eventually, after Hubbard improved his technique to White's satisfaction, he was permitted to play the trumpet that was given to him by a schoolmate, Albert Moore.

During the 1960s, Hubbard's star ascended as he performed with some of the greatest jazz groups of the period. He joined Art Blakey's Jazz Messengers and occupied the chair of departed trumpeter Lee Morgan. In the mid-1960s, Hubbard worked steadily with drummer Max Roach and tenor saxophonist Sonny Rollins. With the momentum generated by his association with such icons of jazz, Hubbard continued to rise, and by the early 1970s, he was among the top jazz trumpeters in the world. His 1972 album *First Light* won a Grammy for best jazz performance of the year. Hubbard died on December 29, 2008, in Sherman Oaks, California.

The Crispus Attucks music department produced a great trombonist who introduced the trombone as a legitimate jazz instrument that thrilled jazz aficionados wherever he performed. He was internationally hailed as one of the greatest trombonist of all times according to jazz polls in the various jazz magazines. James Louis Johnson was born on January 22, 1924, in Indianapolis to

James Horace Johnson and Nina Geiger Johnson. His mother recognized his love for music and hired a piano instructor for his earliest music classes when he was eleven years old. A few years later, in school, he played the baritone saxophone for a short time, but when he was fourteen, he switched to the trombone and formed a band with some of his friends. "We'd get together and just kind of jam," he told National Public Radio. "And [we] needed a trombone player, and so I tried the trombone out and got to fill the gap."[8] He listened to other trombonists, including Fred Beckett and Dickie Wells. Johnson also played trombone in the Crispus Attucks High School band and the Senate Avenue YMCA marching band.

In September 1941, Johnson ventured onto Indiana Avenue and got his first formal engagement with the Clarence Love Orchestra of Kansas City. In March of the following year, he joined the "Snookum" Russell Orchestra, with Ray Brown on bass and Fats Navarro, Tommy Turrentine, and Herbie Phillips on trumpet. The band broke up in October, and Johnson returned home from its national tour. When Benny Carter visited Indianapolis a few days later, he was in need of a trombone player, and Johnson was recommended by entertainment promoter and night club owner Sea Ferguson.

Johnson remained with the Benny Carter Orchestra for the next two years, and in 1944, he traveled to Los Angeles and performed in the Jazz at the Philharmonic Concert. Over the next several years, on different occasions, he played with bandleaders Count Basie and Illinois Jacquet, trumpeter Dizzy Gillespie, and saxophonist Charlie "Bird" Parker. Between 1949 and 1950, he recorded with trumpeter Miles Davis on the legendary *Birth of the Cool* sessions. During this period, Johnson took his artistry in a more creative direction—some would say avant garde—and began to explore the outer limits of jazz. He performed with the leading jazz greats of this period and developed a new perspective on jazz.

> It was in this heady atmosphere that Johnson made a major creative step as he became involved in third-stream composition [a music genre that is a fusion of jazz and classical music—the term was coined in 1957 by composer Gunther Schuller in a lecture at Brandeis University], an engagement that can be traced to his earlier association with Miles Davis and Gil Evans in the Birth of the Cool sessions. Now he was hanging out with a distinctive coterie of musicians who gravitated to Gil's place "a room in a basement on 55th Street, near 5th Avenue . . . behind a Chinese laundry and (with) all the pipes for the building as well as a sink, a bed, a piano, a hot plate and no heat."[9]

Commenting on his escape from rigid rules of jazz interpretation and time-honored convention, Johnson explained his new orientation to David Whiteis

in the April 1995 edition of *Downbeat* magazine: "I know of no reason why jazz
... should sit down in a little corner and behave itself, and never venture out
in any direction, and never be 'bad,' and never be 'annoying,' and 'Mind your
manners!'"[10] Johnson was elected to the *Downbeat* Jazz Hall of Fame in 1995
and retired from performing in 1997. James Louis Johnson died on February 4,
2001, in Indianapolis.

Several Crispus Attucks High School products of music educator Russell
Brown developed their craft in town and took their gifts to the West Coast.
Oregon was one of the destinations. Along with guitarist Wes Montgomery,
pianist Carl Perkins, and drummer Willis Kirk, they made lasting impressions
on the jazz scene and made Indianapolis a household name in the lexicon of
jazz. As far as Leroy Vinnegar was concerned, he came to Portland, Oregon, he
observed the fledgling jazz scene, and he conquered it with his fantastic "walking bass style" of play.

Leroy Vinnegar was a fabulous Indianapolis jazz musician who made Indianapolis and Crispus Attucks High School proud. He was born on July 13, 1928,
to Aaron and Helen Vinnegar in Indianapolis. As a child, he amused himself
by playing the piano in the house, but early on he did not take the instrument
seriously. Some teased him that his large hands were an impediment to his
ambition to learn to play the piano. Eventually, Vinnegar was introduced to the
bass and was instructed by legendary pianist Erroll "Groundhog" Grandy, who
became Vinnegar's primary teacher and mentor. Grandy taught him concepts
and techniques of playing bass lines and hired him for his gigs. Other Indiana
Avenue musicians hired him in their groups, and he became recognized for his
big band sound.

In 1952, at the age of twenty-four, Vinnegar moved to Chicago and won a seat
as the house bass player at the Beehive Jazz Club and backed touring and local
artists such as saxophonist Charlie "Bird" Parker. Two years later, he headed
to Los Angeles and gained a considerable reputation among jazz aficionados
with his unique style of playing the bass—a big band sound with steady walking bass accompaniment and solo patterns. He became a sideman favorite and
performed with stars such as trumpeters Chet Baker and Shorty Rogers; saxophonists Herb Geller, Serge Chaloff, Art Pepper, and Harold Land; and pianists
Russ Freeman and Carl Perkins, who was also originally from Indianapolis.

Vinnegar considered Erroll Grandy and Carl Perkins geniuses and his favorite piano players. He was a bandmate of Carl Perkins at Crispus Attucks
High School and knew of the artistic impact of Erroll Garner when they both
performed in the numerous hot and steamy nightclubs on Indiana Avenue.
Vinnegar observed as Perkins and Garner battled on the keyboards during the

competitive "cutting contest" that pitted one jazz performer against the other as patrons cheered uproariously. He marveled at their similar styles and sought them for performances wherever he performed. The crowning achievement of his extensive recording career, in which he recorded 142 records, was his collaboration with Andre Previn and Shelley Manne on the best-selling album *My Fair Lady*, a jazz version of tunes from the Broadway show. The album was released in 1956 on Lester Koenig's influential West Coast–based Contemporary Records jazz label. This was his first million-selling album.

In 1957, Vinnegar made his debut as a jazz bandleader with his release of the *Leroy Walks* album, which was followed by *Leroy Walks Again* six years later. Both albums were critically acclaimed and featured Vinnegar's uncanny ability to walk his instrument through intricate bass lines. He then teamed up with saxophonist Teddy Edwards in the early 1960s and produced the classic *Teddy's Ready* with Joe Castro on piano and Billy Higgins on drums, and in 1969 he joined pianist Les McCann and saxophonist Eddie Harris on their classic album *Swiss Movement*.

In 1986, health issues forced Vinnegar to relocate to Portland, Oregon, where he became a central figure on the local jazz scene and added an element of authenticity to the city's jazz ambience. He performed at many of the leading jazz clubs and restaurants around town and attracted the attention of up-and-coming jazz students. They frequently sought him out for technical instruction and lessons in jazz history. "Vinnegar was one of the mainstays of jazz all over the world. All I can do is think about the happiness he brought to people when he was playing. Every time he played at the Opus Club, the place was packed and it was stomping. You could always count on him to be swinging and that's what jazz is about. Let me put it this way: jazz equals swing; swing equals Leroy Vinnegar."[11] This statement is from Dick Berk, a jazz drummer who played with Billie Holiday and later worked with Vinnegar in Portland.

The Oregon legislature proclaimed Leroy Vinnegar Day on May 1, 1995, in a special ceremony at the state capitol. He was installed as the first inductee into the Oregon Jazz Society Hall of Fame in 1998. Vinnegar died August 2, 1999, in Portland, and in honor of his great contribution to jazz and his legacy, Portland State University established the Leroy Vinnegar Jazz Institute.

A member of the most popular family of musicians on Indiana Avenue in the 1940s and 1950s, all of whom played one or more instruments, one jazz star emerged from the constellation of his family's orbit and distinguished himself in the world of jazz. Locksley Wellington Slide Hampton was born on April 21, 1932, in Jeanette, Pennsylvania, to Clark Fielding "Deacon" Hampton and Laura Burford-Hampton. He was the youngest of twelve children, all of whom played at least one instrument. In addition to receiving musical instruction in his home, he attended the McArthur Conservatory of Music and was personally instructed by the proprietor, Ruth McArthur, and Eugene Franzman, woodwind instructor and member of the Indianapolis Symphony Orchestra. Although Hampton was right-handed, he was given a trombone set up to play left-handed.

In 1944, he played with the Duke Hampton Band, composed of his siblings, and eight years later, he performed with the Lionel Hampton Orchestra at Carnegie Hall in New York. In the late 1950s, Hampton joined the Maynard Ferguson Band and not only performed but also arranged popular songs such as "Slide's Derangement," "Three Little Foxes," and "The Fugue." In the early 1960s, he organized the Slide Hampton Octet, which featured trumpeters Booker Little and Freddie Hubbard along with saxophonist George Coleman.

In 1968, Slide played with the Woody Herman Orchestra, and afterward, he resided in Europe for almost a decade. He returned to the United States in 1981 and became artist-in-residence at Harvard University; he later held the same position at the University of Massachusetts and DePaul University in Chicago. In 2009, he wrote a composition titled "A Tribute to African-American Greatness," which honored South African president Nelson Mandela, US president Barack Obama, television talk show host Oprah Winfrey, and international tennis star Serena Williams.

Arguably one of the most outstanding jazz scholars and professors of music in the world is an Indianapolis product trained in the music department of Crispus Attucks High School. The Crispus Attucks music department not only produced jazz greats on the bandstand, but also jazz scholars in the classroom. During a period in which some might have separated the elements of jazz performance from jazz history, others might have envisioned a symbiotic relationship between these two elements. One such student who brilliantly combined both elements and quieted all skeptics was internationally known in both categories. David Nathaniel Baker Jr. (fig. 21.1) was born on December 21, 1931, to David Baker Sr. and Patress Baker. He received his earliest music instruction at Francis W. Parker School 56, under the supervision of Clara Kirk and Clarrisa Winlock. He later attended John Hope Franklin School 26, where he studied under Dr. Roscoe Polin, who encouraged him to sing in the school choir. His earliest recollection of music with Polin was performing in the Christmas program. He clearly remembered singing, "Angels We Have Heard on High."

In 1945, Baker entered Crispus Attucks High School, where he began instrumental music instruction under Russell Brown. His first choice of instrument was a tuba, but unfortunately the school did not have one in its inventory. Being an industrious and precocious student, Baker constructed a makeshift tuba

Fig. 21.1 David Baker, professor of jazz studies, Jacobs School of Music at Indiana University. Courtesy of Indiana Historical Society.

from a cigar box and fishing string so that he could practice the fingering techniques. He came to class armed with his homemade contraption, played it, and sang the tuba's music parts. Brown recognized Baker's determination, obtained a sousaphone, and presented it to his creative student.

In the 1940s, a new music genre was born: bebop. Jazz pioneers such as Charlie Parker on alto saxophone, Dizzy Gillespie on trumpet, Thelonious Monk and Bud Powell on piano, Clifford Brown on trumpet, and Coleman Hawkins on tenor saxophone were innovators in this new art form, which swept the nation.

In 1950, Baker entered the Arthur Jordan Conservatory of Music and studied the baritone horn for one year. The following year, he enrolled in Indiana University intending to study to become a classical trombonist and received his bachelor's degree in 1952 and his master's degree in 1954.

The preparation that Baker received under the tutelage of Russell Brown prepared him to venture into Indianapolis nightlife and to meet new challenges. He transitioned from the tuba to the trombone and was anxious to test the water. Among his first engagements were performances at the Sixteenth Street Tavern and the Nineteenth Hole with either Tiny Adams or Mingo Jones on bass, Earl Van Riper on piano, and Robert "Sonny" Johnson on drums. Later, he traveled to California and joined the Stan Kenton Orchestra—he and Curtis Counce became its first African American band members.

In 1959, Gunther Schuller of the Metropolitan Opera Orchestra of New York witnessed a performance of Baker's orchestra in Bloomington and offered him a scholarship to study at the Lenox School of Jazz in Lenox, Massachusetts. Baker studied with a wide range of master teachers, performers, and composers, including trombonist J. J. Johnson, cellist Janos Starker, and composer and bandleader George Russell. He became an award-winning performer, composer, and educator who was nominated for a Pulitzer Prize in 1973 and a Grammy in 1979 and who won an Emmy in 2003. He performed around the world. David Nathaniel Baker died on March 26, 2016, in Bloomington, Indiana.[12]

There were many jazz fans who frequented the clubs on Indiana Avenue and were mesmerized by the creativity and spirituality of the art form. This exposure allowed them to transfer the language of the jazz idiom from the bandstand to the poetry book. One such personality, who was a fan of the Wes Montgomery jazz influence, developed her skills in an equally creative art form. Mari Evans was born Mary Evans to William R. Evans and Mary Evans on July 16, 1919, in Toledo, Ohio. Her mother died when she was just ten years old, and her father encouraged her love of the written word. She studied fashion design at the University of Toledo.

After moving to Indianapolis in the 1940s, she was employed at the Fort Benjamin Harrison Finance Center, and she continued her love of the arts by reading books of many genres. She wrote poetry and short stories and shopped around for a publisher for her material. Her early books were highly acclaimed by the local artistic and historical communities, and she continued to pursue her craft. Her local fame grew, and she was recognized among national scholars as an exceptional poet and writer. She focused her writing on African American arts and literature and eventually gained a series of teaching appointments at various universities, including Indiana University–Purdue University at Indianapolis and Indiana University in Bloomington, Indiana. She lectured at a number of other universities, including Washington University in Saint Louis; Cornell University in Ithaca, New York; the State University of New York–Albany; Northwestern University in Evanston, Illinois; and Spellman College in Atlanta, Georgia. Evans received honorary degrees from Marian College (now Marian University), Martin University, Indiana University, Butler University, and Indiana University–Purdue University at Indianapolis.

From 1968 to 1973, Evans produced, wrote, and directed the television program *The Black Experience* for WTTV, a television station in Indianapolis. Evans published her first work, *Where Is All the Music?*, in 1969. Her most renowned book of poetry, *I am a Black Woman*, was published in 1970. She edited the acclaimed anthology *Black Women Writers (1950–1980): A Critical Evaluation*, which was published in 1984.

In addition, she authored numerous books and essays and contributed to many anthologies and textbooks. Her other books include *Nightstar* (1981); *A Dark and Splendid Mass* (1992); *Continuum: New and Selected Poems* (1997; 2014); *Clarity of Concept: A Poet's Perspective* (2006); and six books for children, including one on teen pregnancy.

Her book *Continuum* included a foreword by the late Maya Angelou and an "After Poem" by Nikki Giovanni. Evans wrote a musical play, an adaptation of Zora Neale Hurston's *Their Eyes Were Watching God* called *Eyes*, as well as what she called a *choreo-poem*, "River of My Song," and a one-woman play, *Boochie*. She served as a consultant for the National Endowment of the Arts from 1969–1970 and was given the National Endowment of the Arts Award for Creative Writing for 1981–1982. Because of her, the celebration of Indianapolis fine arts reached the shores of East Africa; the country of Uganda honored her with a postage stamp in 1997.

In 2001 at the Forty-Fourth Grammy Awards, she collaborated with Jamaican American singer, actor, songwriter, and civil rights activist Harry Belafonte and wrote liner notes for *The Long Road for Freedom: An Anthology of Black Music*. It was nominated in the Best Historical Album category.[13]

THE INDIANA AVENUE JAZZ CONNECTION/ CRISPUS ATTUCKS/McARTHUR CONSERVATORY/THE EXODUS

ALTHOUGH INDIANAPOLIS HAD GAINED PROMINENCE in the world of jazz and the fine arts, there were still barriers to overcome. For decades, Indianapolis jazz greats had been overshadowed by the "Birthplace of Jazz" title bestowed upon New Orleans because of early jazz personalities like bandleader and cornetist Charles "Buddy" Bolden, bandleader King Oliver, and trombonist Louis Armstrong. Indianapolis musicians wanted to continue the march of artistic authenticity and the "war of inclusion" waged by earlier jazz greats primarily associated with Indiana Avenue. The baton of struggle was passed on to a younger group of jazz musicians, and they continued to strive toward empowerment and recognition in the city. Segregation laws pertaining to entertainment were slowly dismantled, but many youngsters left town to find more opportunities. Jazz clubs in neighboring cities like Chicago, Detroit, and Cincinnati were more receptive to African Americans, and the performers were aware of this fact.

Jazz great Wes Montgomery had relocated to Los Angeles, and Freddie Hubbard, Larry Ridley, and James Spaulding had moved to New York. They were determined to be respected in their genre and felt that Indianapolis was incapable of providing the necessary welcome mat.

A young Crispus Attucks High School jazz student who lived in the Lockefield Gardens Public Housing Development that bordered Indiana Avenue was Virgil Jones Jr. He was born on August 16, 1939, to Virgil Jones Sr. and Lucille Lucas-Jones. Growing up, he was constantly exposed to the various kinds of music emanating from Indiana Avenue entertainment establishments. Jones attended William D. McCoy School 24 and then Booker T. Washington School 17, where he met music teacher Russell Brown, who was the music educator at

Fig. 22.1 Wes Montgomery, internationally known guitarist. Courtesy of Indiana Historical Society.

Crispus Attucks. Brown was amazed at Jones's perfect pitch on his trumpet but insisted that he read music well. Jones related, "He must have been a good teacher, because I never had a private teacher and I sight read very well."[1]

In 1952, Jones entered Crispus Attucks High School and joined the band and orchestra under Brown. He became an outstanding honor roll student who scored in the upper 10 percent of the National Scholastic Achievement Examination. At the age of fifteen, Jones refused a four-year genius science scholarship to Morehouse College in Atlanta, Georgia, preferring to graduate from Crispus

Attucks High School. During his senior year, trombonist David Baker was a student teacher at Crispus Attucks, and the relationship between the two became very significant in Jones's jazz career.

During his formative years as a musician, he went to Jacque Durham's Missile Room, near Indiana Avenue, and listened attentively to the up-and-coming jazz guitarist Wes Montgomery (fig. 22.1). Jones related that the most enjoyable aspect of his early music education was jamming at George's Bar and other Indiana Avenue nightspots. Referring to his musical experience, he said, "Many of us would travel to Chicago to hear such popular jazz musicians as trumpeters Miles Davis and Kenny Dorham, tenor saxophonists John Coltrane and Hank Mobley, drummer Max Roach and Philly Joe Jones and bassists Paul Chambers and George Morrow."[2]

After high school graduation, his first gig was playing in the David Baker Big Band at the French Lick, Indiana, Jazz Festival in 1958. Two years later, Baker recommended him to orchestra leader Lionel Hampton, and he joined the orchestra. In 1960, Jones traveled with the Hampton Orchestra to New York and later toured the United States, Europe, Argentina, and Japan. Some of Jones's earliest recordings were on Milt Jackson's *Invitation* album in 1962, Roland Kirk's *Reeds and Deeds* in 1963 and *Slightly Latin* in 1966, and Charles Earland's *Black Talk* in 1969.

Jones expanded his entertainment horizon and explored different arenas, such as Broadway productions, television, and the cabaret circuit. In 1973, he played in the house band that backed Hollywood actress Debbie Reynolds in her Broadway debut of *Irene*. He also provided music for such Broadway hits as *Ain't Misbehavin'*, *Jelly's Last Jam*, and *Big Time Buck White*, which starred world heavyweight boxing champion Muhammad Ali, as well as *Black and Blue*, which highlighted the return of rhythm-and-blues diva Ruth Brown to the bright lights of Broadway.

For seven years, he performed with cabaret singer and pianist Bobby Short at the Carlyle Hotel in New York City and was also a member of the house band for the televised *Dick Cavett Show* for the American Broadcasting Company. Later, Jones performed at the White House during the Bill Clinton administration. In the 1990s, he performed with the Smithsonian Jazz Works Orchestra under the baton of David Baker. Jones died on April 20, 2012, in New York

The Lockefield Gardens public housing development was home to another student of jazz and friend of Virgil Jones who distinguished in the world of jazz. Although he did not attend Crispus Attucks High School, he was greatly influenced by the jazz ambiance for which that entertainment strip was famous. Laurence "Larry" Howard Ridley II was born on September 3, 1937, to Laurence Ridley and Nevoleane Morris-Ridley in Indianapolis. His family loved jazz and other genres of music, all of which he heard constantly in his home. Young Ridley was first inspired to learn the violin through hearing Jascha Heifetz on the *Bell Telephone Hour* radio program in 1942, and the news of his desire to study and play music spread throughout the family. Fortunately, he had a relative who was employed by Pearson's Music Store, and this enabled Ridley's mother to purchase his first musical instrument, a small violin, for ten dollars. He took music lessons from Ruth McArthur, proprietor of the McArthur Conservatory of Music, who charged his mother seventy-five cents per lesson.

Ridley's first road gig was at age sixteen, playing with trumpeter Conte Candoli, who put together a quintet with Slide Hampton on trombone and piano, Benny Barth on drums, Ridley on bass, and Al Kiger on piano. They played nightly for a few months at the Club Shaeferee in South Bend, Indiana. In 1955, after graduating from Shortridge High School, Ridley, with the assistance of music educator Dr. Roscoe Polin, obtained a violin scholarship at the Indiana University School of Music in Bloomington, Indiana.

While attending Indiana University, Ridley formed a jazz quartet with Joe Hunt on drums, Paul Plummer on tenor saxophone, and Austin Crowe on piano, traveled to Indianapolis, and performed at the immensely popular Clown's Playhouse on the south side of the city. Later he joined the David Baker Orchestra.

Gunther Schuller, of the Metropolitan Opera Orchestra of New York, visited Indiana University in 1959 and witnessed Ridley's performance with the David Baker Orchestra. Schuller offered Ridley, Baker, and pianist Al Kiger scholarships to further their jazz studies at the Lenox School of Jazz in Lenox, Massachusetts. There, they studied with pianist, composer, and theorist George Russell, jazz critic and musicologist Marshall Stearns, trumpeter Kenny Dorham, composer and arranger Bill Russo, drummer Max Roach, pianist Bill Evans, and other great musicians.

Ridley completed his undergraduate degree in music at New York University and his master's degree at the State University of New York/Empire State College and received an honorary doctor of performing arts degree at the University of Maryland Eastern Shore. From 1971 until 1999, he was professor of music at Rutgers, the state university of New Jersey, and served as chairman of the Music Department at Rutgers/Livingston College and chief architect of the Jazz Performance Degree Programs at both institutions.

The third jazz notable of the Lockefield Gardens public housing development jazz triumvirate lived in proximity to both Virgil Jones and Larry Ridley. All three jazz men occasionally practiced and played together in impromptu jazz jam sessions around Indiana Avenue. James Ralph Spaulding Jr. was born in Indianapolis on July 30, 1937, to James Ralph Spaulding Sr. and Mae Paul Flournoy Spalding. He was constantly exposed to jazz and swing music, and his father was a professional jazz guitarist who traveled throughout the state and country with the Brown Buddies. This group comprised former Crispus Attucks High School music students, who had named themselves in honor of their beloved music instructor, Harold Brown. (Harold Brown is not to be confused with Russell Brown who was band director when Spauling attended. Harold Brown was an earlier educator.)

His father brought home the most outstanding and popular records of the day, featuring notables such as tenor saxophonists Charlie Parker and Lester Young and vocalists Billie Holiday, Nat King Cole, and Billy Eckstein, and discussed the various elements of their musical style with his wide-eyed, inquisitive son.

Upon entering Crispus Attucks High School, Spaulding enrolled in music courses and met band director Russell Brown. Brown saw so much promise in young Spaulding's music ability that he convinced him to join the band. Spaulding fondly remembered the time and commitment that Russell Brown invested in each music student at Crispus Attucks: "Russell Brown very graciously and unselfishly gave of his time to all of his students that were so inclined to remain after school to play music."[3] Those students included Albert Walton on piano and Virgil Jones and David Hardiman on trumpet. Albert Walton taught Spaulding the saxophone fingering techniques. Spaulding entered military service in 1955 and was stationed at Fort Benjamin Harrison in Indianapolis, where he traveled to Indiana Avenue during the weekends to perform.

While in the army, Larry Ridley recruited Spaulding to play flute and alto and tenor saxophones with jazz contemporaries Freddie Hubbard on trumpet, Larry Ridley on bass, Paul Parker on drums, and Walter Miller and later Al Plank on piano. Ridley desperately needed Spaulding to occupy the saxophone chair to ensure the creativity of the group, so he devised an ingenious plan. Ridley advertised the group's engagement in the *Indianapolis Recorder*, listed all of the musicians by name, and then added a special guest, "Brother Spee Abdul Malik." That was the pseudonym Spaulding employed so that the military would not be aware of his nocturnal moonlighting. They performed to standing-room-only engagements at George's Orchid Room, on Indiana Avenue.

In 1962, Spaulding arrived in New York City and made his first recording as a sideman on a Freddie Hubbard album titled *Hub Tones* on the Blue Note label. He also played with pianist Randy Weston and drummer Max Roach. In the late 1960s, Spaulding attended Livingston College and Rutgers University, where he taught flute as an adjunct professor and became a member of the Duke Ellington Orchestra before departing to complete his education. He performed his original music, a suite titled *A Song of Courage*, with a complete orchestra and choir at the Vorhees Chapel at Rutgers University.

Spaulding was a member of the Freddie Hubbard Quintet, the Sun Ra Arkestra, the Duke Ellington Big Band, the David Murray Octet and Big Band, and the World Saxophone Quartet.

During his long career, the range of his performance experience extended nationally and internationally. He appeared at the Montpelier and Saalfelden Jazz Festivals and recorded on more than one hundred albums with legendary musicians ranging from Louis Armstrong to Sun Ra. He appeared on the Blue Note label with artists such as tenor saxophonists Wayne Shorter, Hank Mobley, Stanley Turrentine, and Sam Rivers and pianists Horace Silver, McCoy Tyner, and Duke Pearson. In 2000, Spaulding recorded three live albums with his band at the Up and Over Jazz Café in Brooklyn, New York, under his own label, Speetones: *Music Volume One, Blues Up and Over Volume Two,* and *Round to It.*

Crispus Attucks High School and Indiana Avenue were not the sole locations where jazz stars cut their proverbial teeth. Jazz was so powerful that its tentacles wrapped around neighborhoods all over the city. Phillip Arthur Ranelin was born on May 25, 1939, to Kenneth Edwin Ranelin and Vera Smith Ranelin in Indianapolis. The person with the most profound influence on his musical career was his paternal grandmother, Helen Kimbrough Ranelin Crawford. She was a quintessential lover of fine music who enjoyed many of the jazz performances at the Sunset Terrace Ballroom on Indiana Avenue. Often, she reminisced of her delight seeing such jazz luminaries as tenor saxophonist Charlie Parker, bandleaders and pianists Duke Ellington and Count Basie, and trumpeters Dizzy Gillespie and Miles Davis perform live. She possessed an extensive record collection consisting of American music of various genres and exposed young Ranelin to the world of jazz at a very early age. Undoubtedly, Ranelin developed an intense appreciation and deep respect for jazz and other forms of American music by witnessing the joy that it provided for his grandmother.

Ranelin received his earliest music education at Hazel Hart Hendricks School 37, where he was initially and briefly instructed by Larry Liggett and then, for the remainder of his music education, by Reginald DuValle Jr. He felt fortunate to have had a music instructor whose specialty was his chosen instrument, the trombone. Recalling DuValle, Ranelin remembered, "As an instructor, he was not intense . . . very much laid back and a smart dresser, but he gave me a firm foundation on the instrument. It was a blessing having Mr. DuValle as my instructor."[4]

Although Ranelin attended Arsenal Technical High School and participated in many facets of its music program, he was greatly indebted to Russell Brown of Crispus Attucks High School's Music Department for challenging him to be the best music student possible by giving him private instruction.

In 1952, while Ranelin was in grade school, along with other aspiring music students, he attended a summer session at Crispus Attucks High School with Russell Brown. "He was great . . . the ultimate educator, quite a performer with a spectacularly advanced knowledge of music. . . . He really could communicate with young people," Ranelin recalled.[5]

In 1957, Ranelin graduated from high school, and the following summer, he sought further music instruction from jazz trombonist David Baker, who gave him private music lessons in his home. "He was very intense . . . very demanding and laid a lot of information on me,"[6] Ranelin noted. In addition to this instruction, Ranelin briefly studied under George Rhodes, the principal trombonist of the Indianapolis Symphony Orchestra at Butler University's Jordan Conservatory of Music.

In 1960, Ranelin relocated to Detroit to explore new horizons. He faced new challenges in the world of jazz, became a fixture on the jazz circuit, and appeared with various musicians in many of the city's hot jazz spots. He reunited with pianist Earl Van Riper and bassist Mingo Jones, both members of the Wes Montgomery Trio, with whom he had previously performed in Indianapolis.

In 1977, Ranelin moved to Los Angeles and immediately hooked up with trumpeter Freddie Hubbard, his music classmate from Arsenal Technical High School. Hubbard received rave reviews in the world of jazz after he recorded his Grammy-winning album *First Light*. Hubbard took Ranelin under his wing, and they performed with another Indianapolis jazz personality, bassist Kent Brinkley, at the popular Roxy nightclub located on Sunset Strip.

Ranelin performed for many years in Los Angeles's hottest jazz nightspots and recorded many highly acclaimed albums, gaining a solid reputation in the world of jazz. In respect for his performing excellence, on November 11, 1999, the mayor and city council of Los Angeles, with an official resolution, designated him as a "Rare and Valuable Cultural Treasure" and a "Cultural Ambassador throughout the Nation and to the World Audience."

Wes Montgomery was undoubtedly the greatest jazz personality produced on Indiana Avenue. He often performed with his brothers, Monk, a bassist who popularized the electric bass guitar and possibly the first jazz performer to be recorded when he jammed with the Art Farmer Septet in 1953, and Buddy Montgomery, a vibraphonist and pianist who played behind blues shouter Big Joe Turner and fellow Indianapolis jazz icon trombonist Slide Hampton. Both brothers formed a jazz aggregation that was very popular. In the mid-1950s, the Mastersounds were an Indianapolis-based jazz quartet featuring Monk Montgomery on the electric Fender bass, Buddy Montgomery on vibes, Benny Barth on drums, and Richie Crabtree on piano. In the winter of 1957, Indianapolis jazz bassist Leroy Vinnegar called Dick Brock, president of World Pacific Records, and said, "I have a tape I want you to hear. It's a terrific group."[7] It was as simple as that. Bock heard the group, and the album *Jazz Showcase Introducing the Mastersounds* was released in 1957. In the liner notes for this album, Ralph J. Gleason, *Downbeat* jazz critic provided the following biographical sketch:

> In the winter of 1956, Williams Howard "Monk" Montgomery returned to his native Indianapolis for a visit. He had been living in Seattle for a few months following several years on the road with the Lionel Hampton orchestra. With Hampton Monk played bass—fender bass, that electronic, over-sized guitar–shaped bass. When Monk came back from Seattle he was burning with the idea of starting a jazz group. He and his brother Charles Frederick "Buddy" Montgomery had always wanted to do this and on that winter 1956 visit, they decided to go ahead. For drummer, they chose another Indianapolis player, Ben Caldwell Barth, who had played with them previously. For piano, they sought out Richard Arthur Crabtree whom they remembered from jam sessions when Johnny "Scat" Davis band had passed through town.[8]

So the Mastersounds were born. The name, incidentally, was suggested by Buddy Montgomery's wife, Lois Ann. Monk, from his experience in Seattle, was convinced a good jazz group would have a chance to work in that city, and he was right. On January 14, 1957, they opened a three-month engagement at Dave's Blue Room in Seattle, Washington. "The whole idea was Buddy's," Monk says, "with each man in charge of one department."[9] Monk, for instance, acted as spokesman for the others; Richie handled the book work and the uniforms; Buddy set the tempo and called the tunes, and Benny was in charge of the rehearsals, among other duties. The group's next album, *The King and I: A Jazz Interpretation by the Mastersounds,* based on Rodgers and Hammerstein's Broadway play, was also released in 1957. The Mastersounds disbanded as a performing group in 1969.[10]

—ᴠᴠ—

HISTORIC FIRSTS OF THE 1960s AND THEIR MOVERS AND SHAKERS

THE INDEPENDENCE OF SEVERAL AFRICAN nations, including Ghana in 1957, Senegal and Nigeria in 1960, and Kenya in 1963, instilled a great deal of pride in African Americans in Indianapolis. Generationally, many Blacks had been raised with negative stereotypes and a deliberately distorted history of Africa. Interestingly, these images were advanced by depictions in the majority media, such as Hollywood motion pictures, books, and carnival attractions. In essence, Hollywood played a major role in the propagation of the racist, negative, and inaccurate images inherent in the description of Africa as the "Dark Continent."

Many Lockefield Gardens youngsters flocked to the Walker Theatre on steamy Saturday mornings to catch the nine-cent action movies. They sat glued to the edges of their seats, devouring hot dogs and popcorn as Johnny Weissmuller portrayed Edgar Rice Burroughs's titular character *Tarzan of the Jungle* on the silver screen. Dressed only in a leopard-skin loincloth, he swung on vines through the African jungle and dominated the so-called "African natives" with his red-haired, blue-eyed mate, Jane (Brenda Joyce). He was stronger, smarter, wiser, and more athletic than anyone on the African continent.

Tarzan communicated with animals of the jungle, but the "natives" did not have the intellectual capacity to do so. African American youth identified with him as he battled African "natives" in many of the war scenes. He represented heroism and virtue, and the African "natives" represented savagery and barbarism.

These images shaped the minds of some young African Americans who considered themselves as racially inferior, and to some extent, the depictions cemented their identity. Weissmuller subliminally defined in those young minds the power equation in America.

During the early to middle 1960s, the Indiana State Fair also played a role in the propagation of negative images in the African American community. It featured a carnival attraction billed as the "Wild Lady from the Jungles of Darkest Africa," which was very popular among carnival patrons. People stood in long lines to purchase tickets after viewing the colorful advertisement murals on the front of the show wagon. The images were of half-naked African "natives" being chased by lions and tigers and of coiled cobras ready to make deadly strikes.

Shortly before the "Wild Lady" appeared onstage, the thunder of wooden planks crashing together and a wild, bloodcurdling came from behind the curtains. As the curtains rose, a Black lady appeared in a dark, shadowy cage with images of wild animals in the background. She was dressed in loosely fitted leopard-skin rags. Her eyes gyrated wildly as she moved her neck. Bushy hair covered her head.

With a live chicken clenched between her teeth, she belted out a scream, bit the chicken's neck, and sent blood oozing from her mouth. The carnival barker told viewers that she had been captured deep in the jungles of the Congo and had resided with great apes and monkeys. The crowd erupted in amazement as they viewed this alarmingly exotic spectacle. She was the symbol of Africa to fair patrons of all races, creeds, and colors. African Americans of all ages were reminded that their ancestry was purported to be connected to these stereotypical images of Africa presented by some segments of the American media.[1] African Americans had to discard these racist representations from their minds and develop a positive image. International and national events that occurred around the world gave them a new perspective. It validated their humanity. They saw people who looked like them reach outstanding goals and distinguish themselves in the international community. They reasoned that if those individuals could struggle against racial discrimination and oppression, why couldn't we?

On the front pages of the *Indianapolis Recorder*, African Americans saw people who looked like them untethering themselves from the yokes of European colonialism in Africa and fighting ferociously to choose the course of their lives. Many citizens identified with their struggle and wished to duplicate it in Indianapolis. During these decades, there were historically monumental events advertised throughout the country. Louis Stokes of Cleveland and Richard Hatcher of Gary, Indiana, became the first African American mayors of a major American city.

The eyes of the world focused on Indianapolis when news reports covered the story of heart-transplant recipient Louis B. Russell. On December 3, 1967, less than a year earlier, South African cardiac surgeon Dr. Christian Barnard had performed the world's first heart transplant, placing the heart of accident victim Denise Darvall into the chest of fifty-four-year-old Louis Washkansky.

Russell was born in Terre Haute, Indiana, and graduated from Garfield High School. During World War II, he joined the Army Air Forces. He graduated from Indiana State Teachers College with a Bachelor of Science degree in 1954 and earned a Master of Science degree in industrial education. He was an instructor at the Indiana Boys' School and later taught in the Indianapolis Public School System.

In 1965, Russell suffered one of several heart attacks that ultimately weakened his heart, and he later required a transplant. On August 24, 1968, he received a heart transplant at the Medical College of Virginia Hospital in Richmond, Virginia. The donor, a seventeen-year-old, died as the result of a gunshot wound to the head. Later, Russell traveled the country extensively, delivering speeches about his heart issues and stressing the importance of education to youthful audiences. Russell lived with his transplanted heart for six years and died in November 1974 at the Medical College of Virginia.[2]

Only a few decades away from slavery, African Americans were faced with many obstacles that often involved the legal establishment. Without proper representation, they were at the mercy of unjust laws that made their lives difficult in a sea of racial discrimination. Many did not understand the machinations of the legal system and were at the mercy of unscrupulous lawyers. They were in desperate need of someone like Freeman Briley Ransom to represent their concerns in a court of law.

Freeman Briley Ransom (fig. 23.7) was born on July 7, 1880, to Clem Ransom and Louise/Lula Ransom in Grenada, Mississippi. He attended Walden College in Nashville, Tennessee, a historically Black college founded in 1865 by missionaries from the northern United States on behalf of the Methodist Church. He traveled to New York and completed his law degree at Columbia University.

Ransom relocated to Indianapolis around 1910 and met Madam C. J. Walker, entrepreneur, philanthropist, political and social activist, and owner of the cosmetics and hair-care empire. He became the attorney and business manager of the Madam C. J. Walker Manufacturing Company. Simultaneously, he operated a law firm with partner Robert Lee Brokenburr, who assumed the position of general manager after Ransom's death.

Ransom served as legal counsel for the Senate Avenue YMCA, the Phyllis Wheatley Young Women's Christian Association (YWCA), the Indianapolis branch of the NAACP, and the Frederick Douglass Life Insurance Company. He served on the Indianapolis City Council from 1939 to 1942 and was president of Flanner House, a social service agency. He was one of the founders of the Negro Business League and the Marion County Bar Association. Ransom was an active member of the Bethel AME Church, the Knights of Pythias, and the Good Citizen's League.

Fig. 23.7 Freeman Ransom. Courtesy of Judity Ransom-Lewis.

Ransom and his wife, Nettie Lillian Cox-Ransom, a native of Jackson, Mississippi, had six children: Frank, Frederic, Willard, Robert, Clifford, and A'Lelia (named after the daughter of Madam C. J. Walker). The Ransom family home was located at 828 North California Street, and the surrounding neighborhood was named in honor of Ransom and his wife and designated the Ransom Place Historic District. It was listed on the National Register of Historic Places in 1992. Attorney Freeman Briley Ransom died on August 6, 1947.[3]

Freeman Briley Ransom blazed a trail in the court rooms in Indianapolis that inspired his young son to follow in his footsteps.

Freeman's son, Willard Blystone "Mike" Ransom, was born on May 17, 1916. He was educated in the Indianapolis Public School System and attended the Mary Elizabeth Cable School 4 and the Booker Taliaferro Washington School 17. He graduated from Crispus Attucks High School in 1932 at the age of sixteen and was an honor roll student who excelled academically in the classroom and athletically on the basketball court and football field. He was also a member of the debating team.

He attended Talladega College in Talladega, Alabama, where he majored in history and continued his remarkable level of academic and athletic excellence as a member of the college varsity basketball and football teams and the college debating team. He developed a penchant for William Shakespeare and could perfectly recite passages from many of the masterpieces by rote memory. Ransom was recognized as a college scholar in history and graduated summa cum laude in 1936. His loyalty and pride in his alma mater led him to become one of the founders and leaders in the establishment of regional reunions for alumni of Talladega College.

In 1939, Ransom graduated from the Harvard University School of Law and returned to Indianapolis, where he was employed as a deputy attorney general for the state of Indiana. During World War II, he was inducted into the US Army on June 6, 1941, at Fort Benjamin Harrison in Indianapolis, Indiana. He received training as a pilot at the Edgewood Arsenal Aberdeen Proving Ground in Maryland and then relocated to the Chemical Warfare Division at the Tuskegee Army Airforce Base in Tuskegee, Alabama.

In April 1942, he was one of only two African Americans in the class of forty-one soldiers in the Third Officers Candidate Course. He completed the training, was commissioned as an officer, and rose to the rank of captain. Later, Ransom served as counsel in the Judge Advocate General's Department in France and Belgium.

After his discharge from military service, he returned to Indianapolis and became the manager of the C. J. Walker Manufacturing Company. He married the former Gladys Lucille Miller and became the proud parent of two children, Philip Freeman, a Harvard Law School graduate, and Judith Ellen, a Spelman College graduate.

Returning to Indianapolis after serving his country in the military, Ransom may have questioned some of the elements of the foundation of American democracy, primarily basic civil rights and the *Equal Justice Under the Law* phrase engraved in stone on the front of the US Supreme Court Building in Washington, DC. He may have witnessed "patronage whites only solicited" signs posted on carousels at the Riverside Park Amusement Park; the segregationist policies that prohibited African American patronage at many of the downtown theaters, hotels, and restaurants; the segregation at his beloved Crispus Attucks High School; and the segregation in sports activities around the state.

Ransom took these injustices to heart, recognized the debilitating and demoralizing effects of racism on African Americans in Indianapolis, and became a heavyweight fighter in the Indianapolis political arena. He played a major role in the passage of all significant civil rights legislation since 1946 and coauthored the Indiana Anti-segregation School Law in 1949.

He was co-counsel in the case that eliminated discrimination against African Americans in selection and promotion at the Indianapolis Police and Fire Departments, and he served five terms as president of the NAACP. A few decades later, he was one of the founders of Indiana Black Expo. With the same degree of grit and determination he displayed on the basketball court and football field of Crispus Attucks High School and Talladega College, he fought in the courtrooms and legislatures not only in Indianapolis but throughout the state of Indiana. Attorney Willard Blystone Ransom died on Tuesday, November 7, 1995.[4]

The twentieth century presented many social problems for African Americans in Indianapolis. One such problem was that of medical care. Many of the hospitals were segregated so Black residents had to find other medical alternatives. There was a dire need for medical care with no one to provide this service. Joseph Ward was born on June 4, 1899, to Mittie Ward and Napoleon Hagans in Wilson, North Carolina. He moved to Indianapolis and attended Shortridge High School. He worked as a chauffeur for white physician Dr. George Hasty. According to the July 22, 1899, edition of the *Freeman*, Dr. Hasty expressed his confidence in the ability of young Ward and stated, "There was something unusual in the green looking country boy and to the delight of Joe [as he called him] he offered to send him to school."

Sometime during the 1890s, Ward earned a degree from the Indiana Medical College and practiced medicine in Indianapolis. In 1899, the *Freeman* wrote, "The fact that he has risen from the bottom of poverty, through honorable poverty, without any assistance, is sufficient evidence to justify our belief in his success in the future."[5]

During this period, African Americans were denied treatment in city hospitals, so he opened Ward's Sanitarium and Nurses' Training School at 723 Indiana Avenue. He convinced the administration of the segregated City Hospital to allow his Black nursing students to attend courses, which enabled them to pass the licensing examinations. Dr. Ward became as foundational to Indianapolis's rich Black history as the *Freeman* newspaper publisher George Knox and entrepreneur Madam C. J. Walker, whom Ward helped get their professional start. He was one of the founders of the Senate Avenue YMCA. Dr. Joseph Ward died on December 15, 1956.

Near the turn of the twentieth century, African Americans were cognizant of the fact that many problems experienced by Blacks in the South were social barometers for issues that would ultimately appear in the North. In the January 7, 1899, edition of the *Indianapolis Recorder*, an editorial reflected the concerns that Blacks anticipated. It referenced a racist insurrection in Wilmington, North Carolina, led by Senator John Dillard Bellamy, to suppress the African American vote: "Has it never occurred to the White Press that the intelligent foreigner might think it a little irregular that a United State Senator should advocate the use of shot guns at the polls to prevent Negroes from voting? It still further explains why there is no opposition to the voting of Representative Elect John Dillard Bellamy of North Carolina, who played a conspicuous part in the Wilmington outrage. There is a possibility that the intelligent reader may conceive the idea that the nation is a party to the practice of murdering Negroes." Wilmington lawyer William Henderson was one targeted in the insurrection and wrote of Bellamy, "[He] walks cheerfully to his seat over broken homes, broken hearts, disappointed lives, dead husbands and fathers, the trampled right of freedmen and not one word of condemnation." Effective legal representative was necessary for the enfranchisement for African Americans in Indianapolis. Indianapolis needed a legal champion desperately.

Robert Lieutenant Bailey was born on June 29, 1885, to Robert Bailey and Mary Ann White Bailey in Florence, Alabama. Both parents were former slaves who placed a premium on education and wanted their son to get a quality education so he could improve his position in life. Thanks to the educational initiative of the American Missionary Association—a Protestant-based abolitionist group founded in 1846 that promoted the abolition of slavery, the education of African Americans, racial equality, and Christian values—Bailey attended the Stephen F. Slater School, in Bristol, Tennessee. Slater was a proponent of the association's philosophy, a philanthropist, and an education advocate who opened the school in 1900.[6]

Bailey's academic aptitude was immediately recognized, as he excelled in his early education programs in school. He continued in his quest for educational excellence and was accepted into the High School Division Program at Talladega College in Talladega, Alabama. He completed the program in two years, entered the college program, finished it in three years, and graduated in 1906.

After college, he worked as a federal railway postal clerk in Birmingham, Alabama, while taking correspondence law courses. He was admitted to the Indiana Law School in Indianapolis and completed his Bachelor of Laws (LLB) degree in 1912. The following year, he joined with other Black railway clerks to found the National Alliance of Postal Employees, and he served as their legal counsel and secretary for many years.

Bailey relocated to Indianapolis, collaborated with other Black attorneys such as Robert L. Brokenburr and Freeman B. Ransom, and fought for freedom and justice for African Americans in Indianapolis. He opened an Indianapolis law office with Brokenburr, Ransom, and, later, F. W. Littlejohn. He served as assistant attorney general under James M. Ogden and subsequently as judge pro tem of Marion County Circuit Court for Judge Harry O. Chamberlin. He was a member of both the Indianapolis and Illinois Bar Associations and was president and counsel for the Indianapolis NAACP. Robert Lieutenant Bailey died on March 4, 1940.[7]

The Flanner House social service agency addressed the social needs of African Americans from the beginning of the twentieth century to the present. It had great leaders from the community who saw fit to make this institution a beacon of light for the African American community. Cleo Walter Blackburn (fig. 23.1) was born on September 27, 1909, in Port Gibson, Mississippi. He was the eleventh of twelve children born to David Blackburn, a former slave, and Sarah Blackburn, a minister and a teacher. His grandfather William Blackburn gained his freedom before the Emancipation Proclamation by saving the daughter of the master, and he related to young Blackburn the story of his freedom and his conversation with the slave owner: "William, we'll give you anything that you want, the master promised him. The hero [William] said that he would settle for his freedom, the freedom of his wife and the title to one hundred acres of land."[8]

Blackburn attended the Southern Christian Institute, a boarding school for Black students established by the Christian Church of Saint Edwards, Mississippi, where he received his high school diploma. In 1928, he relocated from his family farm to Indianapolis with only $7.19 in his pocket.

Fig. 23.1 Cleo Blackburn, Flanner House Social Service Agency. Courtesy of Indiana Historical Society.

Undaunted by his meager financial resources, Blackburn was determined to succeed. He worked his way through Butler University and took a series of menial jobs to finance his education. He washed dishes at the Third Christian Church (now Broadway United Methodist Church) and fired the furnaces of large homes near the church for $2.50 per week. On Indiana Avenue, he worked at the Walker Drug Store and Coffee Pot as a janitor for $8 per week and Eaton's Restaurant for $14 per week.

He entered Butler University in 1928 and received a Bachelor of Arts in sociology with a minor from the School of Religion in 1932. Shortly after graduation, he refused a scholarship from the Yale University Divinity School because he did not want to preach.

Blackburn enrolled in the Fisk University Graduate School of Social Work and received his master's degree. He also studied at the Wharton School of the University of Pennsylvania in Philadelphia and later was a Rosenwald Fellow at Indiana University. Throughout his collegiate administrative career, he occupied several prominent positions. He was head of the Department of Sociology and Economics at Knoxville College in Knoxville, Tennessee, and later became head of the Department of Records and Research at Tuskegee Institute in Tuskegee, Alabama. In 1935, he accepted the position of superintendent of the Indianapolis Social Service Agency, Flanner House, and was appointed executive director the following year.

During his tenure with Flanner House, he made outstanding contributions to the African American community in the areas of employment, health services, and housing. During World War II, Flanner House trained more than 1,500 undereducated African Americans for employment in defense plants and other industries.

Later, he recognized the need for health services in the underserved community; the City Hospital had limited facilities, and Methodist Hospital did not admit African Americans. In 1946, the Metropolitan Health and Hospital Corporation joined Flanner House to create the Herman G. Morgan Health Center, and Blackburn was appointed director. From 1947 until 1952, more than five thousand persons received free examinations and medical services at the center.

In 1950, the Flanner House Sweat Equity Program provided housing and homeownership for more than four hundred families, many of whom were first-generation homeowners. The program offered economic stability and a pathway to the middle class.

During this period, Blackburn assumed the position of president of Jarvis Christian College in Hawkins, Texas, for eleven years. He was ordained by the Christian Church Disciples of Christ and pastor of the Lea Avenue Christian

Church. Blackburn retired from Flanner House in 1975 and died on June 1, 1978, in Indianapolis.[9]

From an impoverished childhood as the son of former slaves to aspirations of being Commander in Chief in the White House, Frank Roscoe Beckwith reached for unimaginable goals in life. Indianapolis produced an individual who shed the shackles of mental oppression and overcame ubiquitous road blocks. Frank Roscoe Beckwith (fig. 23.2) was born on December 11, 1904, to Frank Beckwith Sr., the son of former Kentucky slaves, and Lethia Beckwith. The son of his mother's slave master freed her family at the outbreak of the Civil War, when she was two years old, and her father escaped slavery when he was fifteen years old. Beckwith attended Indianapolis Public Schools 37 and 26 and graduated from Arsenal Technical High School in 1921. He received his law school education from the offices of attorneys Sumner A. Clancy and Asa J. Smith. Beckwith published the *Indianapolis Tribune*, an African American newspaper that operated from 1927 to 1938.

He joined the Republican Party in 1928 and served as the director of welfare and safety for the Indiana Industrial Board. In 1935, he challenged the Indiana General Assembly to adopt a law that provided free transportation for Indiana children who attended public schools out of their home school districts.

In 1943, he gave a radio address, "The Negro Lawyer and the War," which was subsequently published by the American Bar Association. Throughout the years, he tested the political waters, and he ran for the state legislature in 1936 and the Indianapolis City Council two years later. Neither bid was successful. He championed the struggle against the Indiana High School Athletic Association to have Crispus Attucks High School admitted as a bona fide member with the right to participate in all sports competitions against other high schools. Previously, Crispus Attucks had been barred from participation in sports events and only played African American or parochial schools. In addition, he courageously fought to increase the hiring of African American police officers, to construct a new community building at Douglass Park, and to construct Lockefield Gardens for low-income families. He also helped African Americans gain employment in the Marion County General Hospital. On August 24, 1965, Frank Roscoe Beckwith died in St. Vincent's Hospital.[10]

Indianapolis was blessed with many brilliant legal minds. One such individual distinguished himself in the community, served well, and made outstanding contributions. Initially he wanted to be a social studies teacher at Crispus Attucks High School, but he was denied the position due to lack of teaching experience. He then chose the career in law and many viewed this as a godsend. Rufus Calvin Kuykendall was born on September 24, 1903, to John H. Kuykendall,

Fig. 23.2 Attorney Frank Beckwith, the first African American to run for the US presidency. Courtesy of Indiana Historical Society.

Fig. 23.3 Ethel Ransom-Kuykendall and Judge Rufus Kuykendall. Courtesy of Indiana Historical Society.

the son of a former slave from Tennessee, and Annabelle Jackson Kuykendall in Indianapolis. In 1921, he attended Indiana University, where he majored in history and political science, and he graduated from the Indiana School of Law in 1942. He was deputy prosecutor for six years and was assistant city attorney under Mayor Archie Clark. He was married to Ethel Ransom-Kuykendall (fig. 23.3). President Dwight David Eisenhower appointed him as a member of the United Nations Educational, Scientific and Cultural Organization (UNESCO). He died on November 4, 1977.[11]

Scholars from outstanding universities around the country relocated to Indianapolis to pursue careers in law. Many were born in the South and recognized the need for legal representation in African American communities throughout the country. One such individual was Mercer Montgomery Mance, born on December 23, 1910, to Robert Weston Mance and Elizabeth Grimes Mance in Beaufort, South Carolina. He completed his grade school and high school education at the Allen University Demonstration School in Columbia, South Carolina, where his father, a minister and educator, was president. The school, cofounded by his grandfather, ensured that young Black children had the opportunity to be educated, and its curriculum included courses from the first grade through college level. Mance graduated from Howard University in 1931 with a bachelor's degree and continued his education at the Harvard University School of Law in Cambridge, Massachusetts, where he received his doctorate in jurisprudence in 1934. He married Mary Kathalyn Stuart-Mance on October 16, 1951, and was the father of two children. He was the first African American elected to the court in Indiana, and in 1958 he was elected to the Superior Court, where he served three terms until 1978. He was a trustee and highly esteemed member of Bethel AME Church. He was an ardent advocate of public school education who believed that "every individual should have the opportunity for quality education that he or she may be advanced to the highest level of their natural capacity for achievement." Mercer Montgomery Mance died on October 17, 1990.[12]

In 1963, the social, political, and economic atmosphere in Indianapolis was thick with toxic dust generated by the events that were reported daily in the news media. That year, the Greensboro Four, David Richmond, Franklin Mc-Cain, Ezell Blair Jr., and Joseph McNeil, students from the North Carolina Agricultural and Technical University, refused to leave a whites-only counter in a Woolworths store in Greensboro, North Carolina. Woolworths and other downtown eating establishments refused to serve African Americans at their lunch counters. Students from several colleges joined forces and staged sit-ins at counters throughout the South. Ultimately, many establishments relented and rescinded their segregationist policies. These demonstrations prompted local community activists and students from Crispus Attucks High School to demonstrate at the Woolworths establishment in downtown Indianapolis.[13]

On June 11, 1963, Alabama governor George Wallace defiantly stood in the doorway of Foster Hall at the University of Alabama and blocked the entrance of two African American students, Vivian Malone and James Hood. Wallace appealed to his base with the promise of "I denounce and forbid this illegal act." In response to Wallace's edict, President John Fitzgerald Kennedy issued Executive Order 11111, which federalized the Alabama National Guard, and Wallace stepped aside, permitting the students to enter the building. This event emboldened local community activists.[14]

On September 15, 1963, four young African American girls, Addie Mae Collins, Cynthia Wesley, Carole Robertson, and Carol Denise McNair, were killed, prior to Sunday service, at the Sixteenth Street Baptist Church in Birmingham, Alabama. Four members of the Ku Klux Klan planted dynamite connected to a timing device beneath the steps of the church. Dr. Martin Luther King Jr. responded by calling it "one of the most vicious and tragic crimes ever perpetrated against humanity."[15] The world looked with horror at images of the church with smoke rising from its ashes and church members wailing in agony and disbelief.

The events of 1963 galvanized the African American community in Indianapolis and forced civic leaders to take a deep, introspective look at the issue of civil rights in the city. On August 3, 1963, a headline in the Indianapolis *Recorder* read "NAACP Host to HUGE RALLY." The article included this statement:

> The NAACP has launched a community-wide call to all fair-minded persons, regardless of race, color or creed to join in the peaceful demonstration to commence at 1:30 pm at the World War Memorial Plaza and terminate at University Park. Greeting will be extended by Governor Matthew E. Welsh, for the state of Indiana, Mayor Albert Losche for the city of Indianapolis, Rabbi Maurice Davis of the Indianapolis Hebrew Congregation, for the Jewish community.... The rally is aimed at voicing the concerns for the grave local unemployment problem of Negro people and demonstration of physical support of federal civil rights legislation now pending in congress.

Demonstrators from many segments of the Indianapolis community marched in a united front to protest many racist elements embedded in the Indianapolis community (fig. 23.4).

April 4, 1968, is recorded as one of the most historically significant days in the annals of Indianapolis history. It was a day similar to that of the John F. Kennedy assassination or the destruction of the Twin Towers on 9/11 in New York City. It is a day about which later generations innocently ask, "Where were you...?" On that day Robert Fitzgerald Kennedy (fig. 23.5), recently arrived from speaking engagements at the University of Notre Dame and Ball State University, driven to a park deep in the African American community of Indianapolis, stood on a podium mounted on a flatbed truck and delivered these words:

> I'm going to talk to you just for a minute or so this evening, because I have some very sad news for all of you ... for all of our fellow citizens and people who love peace all over the world and that is that Martin Luther King was shot and killed tonight in Memphis, Tennessee. Martin Luther King dedicated his life to love and justice between fellow human beings. He died in the cause of that effort. In this difficult day, in this difficult

Fig. 23.4 Civil rights march in downtown Indianapolis, March 1963. Courtesy of Indiana Historical Society.

time for the United States, it's perhaps well to ask what kind of a nation we are, what direction we want to move in. We can move in that direction as a country, in greater polarization black people amongst blacks and white people amongst whites, filled with hatred toward one another. Or we can make an effort, as Martin Luther King did, to understand and to comprehend and replace that violence, that stain of bloodshed that had spread across our land, with an effort to understand, compassion and love.

The death of Martin Luther King illustrated the restraint and patience of Blacks in Indianapolis during this tumultuous period. In cities from coast to coast, riots erupted, people were killed, and neighborhoods and businesses burned to the ground. In Indianapolis, Senator Robert Kennedy's words of comfort averted a deadly riot. Blacks in Indianapolis had come of age.[16]

The name Robert Lee Brokenburr was celebrated in legal communities in Indianapolis and around the state. He was a champion of the downtrodden

Fig. 23.5 Robert Kennedy announcing Martin Luther King Jr.'s assassination to a crowd in Indianapolis. Courtesy of Indiana Historical Society.

and worked tirelessly to improve their living conditions in the city. Robert Lee Brokenburr was born on November 16, 1886, to Benjamin Brokenburr and Mary Elizabeth Baker-Brokenburr in (Phoebus/Chesapeake) Elizabeth City, Virginia. His mother had been taught to read and write and even play the piano by the owners of the farm on which her parents had lived. She was very ambitious for her children.. Because of the good fortune of living near the Whittier Elementary School, Robert, the eldest of nine children, was able to get a sound start in education.

The Whittier School was a prep school for Hampton (Institute) Normal students. He worked his way through the Whittier Elementary School and earned $2.50 a week shaking out laundry. The June 6, 1933, edition of the *Indianapolis Recorder* reported: "In his early boyhood days, he served as a fisherman's helper, sold newspapers, worked in the tailor shop, worked in the hotel laundry and did any kind of odd jobs he could find to earn money to further his education."[17]

Brokenburr continued his education at Hampton Institute, whose philosophy of the importance of hard work, dedication to the uplift of others, and academic excellence was one of the strongest influences of his life. The founder, General Samuel Chapman Armstrong, formerly of the Union Army, called this philosophy "Education for Life," and Brokenburr often spoke of "the Hampton Spirit."

During his tenure at Hampton Institute, he not only played with the band but sang with the Hampton Institute quartet and chorus. Both musical groups often accompanied the president of the school on fundraising campaigns. Because of his travel, often to New England and New York State, it was sometimes his privilege to be on the same stage as an outstanding speaker or public figure of the day, such as African American educator and political leader Booker T. Washington (a Hampton Institute alumnus) and esteemed author Mark Twain. Many of these events took place in Carnegie Hall, New York City.

Brokenburr also began working summers at resorts in Lake George, New York, as a porter. His experiences there broadened his horizons, and he decided, upon graduation from Hampton Institute in 1906, to enroll in the Howard University School of Law in Washington, DC. He graduated in 1909. "It wasn't easy to raise the money for school while living in a city of that size, but I managed, with the diligence and occasional invitations to dinner at the home of an Uncle and Aunt," he mused.

Brokenburr moved to Indianapolis in 1909 and joined the law firm of Freeman B. Ransom. He became a close acquaintance of Madam C. J. Walker, the African American cosmetics entrepreneur regarded as the country's first female millionaire. Along with Ransom, Brokenburr served as general counsel of the

Walker Manufacturing Company. During the 1920s, he worked as the Marion County deputy prosecuting attorney.

In 1940, Brokenburr made history and became the first African American elected to the Indiana Senate. Except for one two-year hiatus, he served continuously until 1964. His work in the civil rights arena included the establishment of fair employment practices; improvement in voter registration and election participation among minorities, brought about by the establishment of an impartial voter registration board; and improvement in opportunities for African Americans to serve in the National Guard.

A member of the National Bar Association, Brokenburr served on the Committee of Jurisprudence and Law Reform, the Publicity Committee, and the Committee on Affiliations of Bar Association. He was active in numerous civic organizations, including the Colored Men's Civic League, the Senate Avenue YMCA, the NAACP, the Hampton Institute Board of Trustees, the United Negro College Fund Board of Directors, and the Flanner House. In 1955, President Eisenhower named him an alternate delegate to the United Nations. He culminated his legislative career by authoring civil rights laws that were passed in 1961 and 1963. Robert Lee Brokenburr died on May 24, 1974, in Indianapolis.[18]

During the turn of the century, Indianapolis desperately needed institutions to help the influx of impoverished former slaves from the South, many of whom required remediation to make a successful transition from the agricultural to the urban community. Of the few social service industries that served the community, the names of Faburn Edward DeFrantz and the Senate Avenue YMCA are inextricably linked to greatness. Faburn Edward DeFrantz was born in Topeka, Kansas, on February 9, 1885, to Alonzo D. and Samella E. DeFrantz. He attended public schools in Topeka and later attended Washburn College, Kansas University, the Kansas Medical College, the Kent Law School, and the Springfield Young Men's Christian Association College. He arrived in Indianapolis in 1912 after a year of employment at the Washington, DC, YMCA.

He was appointed executive secretary of the Senate Avenue YMCA in 1915 and served in that capacity for thirty-six years. DeFrantz was a civil rights trailblazer who spent many years fighting all forms of racial discrimination. He married Myrtle Summers-DeFrantz on June 18, 1917.

DeFrantz believed that for a community to attain greater social, economic, and political power, elements of enlightenment and civil discourse must be injected into the movement. Thomas Taylor, a former executive secretary of the Senate Avenue YMCA, organized a speakers' forum initially named the Big Meeting, which was later changed to the Monster Meeting because of a similarly named annual meeting of the central YMCA board.

Many of the early speakers at the meeting covered topics with a religious theme, but DeFrantz broadened the discourse and invited speakers with additional topics that affected various segments of the community. Some of the speakers included former first lady Eleanor Roosevelt, Olympic track star Jesse Owens, Indiana governor Paul V. McNutt, esteemed scientist Dr. George Washington Carver of Tuskegee Institute, and author Langston Hughes of the Harlem Renaissance.

In October 1924, David Curtis Stephenson, the grand dragon of the Ku Klux Klan, planned a parade down Indiana Avenue in full regalia. According to David DeFrantz, Faburn's grandson, "Granddad approached Stephenson at his headquarters to emphatically demand that the Ku Klux Klan must not march down Indiana Avenue with their hoods. Before DeFrantz could reach Stephenson, a Klan body guard intervened to block DeFrantz. He picked up the body guard and moved him out of the way."

In the October 3, 1964, edition of the *Indianapolis Recorder*, Andrew Ramsey wrote in his column Voice from the Gallery, in reference to DeFrantz's invaluable contributions to the Indianapolis community:

> DeFrantz was quick to see possibilities in the boys who came to the Y M C A and directly, he influenced hundreds to develop their potentialities. Among those he helped on their way are artists, teachers, physicians, dentists, several Ph.D.'s and many outstanding citizens with less glamorous occupations. He prodded but did not preach. His was the magic leadership of the personal touch rather than that of the teachings of the scholar or the exhortation of the orator.
>
> In short, the late F. E. DeFrantz was a leader who felt he was part of the group that he led and who never acquired the messiah complex which so many leaders are prone to adopt. He was a man among men that he led more by example than precept. By training, he was neither a psychologist nor a philosopher, yet he possessed a working knowledge of psychology which would put to shame the academic psychology of many PhD's in the field and he possessed a philosophy about humanity devoid of the obscurantism of the ivory tower. Indianapolis is infinitely richer, because he lived and worked in this city and in his passing, the city, Negroes, and the whole nation have lost one who was a great humanitarian and at the same time, a simple human being who loved humanity in spite of its foibles and its weaknesses.[19]

Faburn Edward DeFrantz died on September 24, 1964.[20]

During the middle of the twentieth century, African Americans needed champions such as Henry Johnson Richardson Jr. to wage war in the arena of equity in public education. Public school segregation was a road block to the realization of providing every student, regardless of race, a quality education. Henry Johnson Richardson Jr. was born on June 21, 1902, to Henry J. Richardson and Louise M. Johnson Richardson in Huntsville, Alabama. His father was a veteran of the Spanish-American War who worked as an insurance agent. His mother worked at home. When Richardson was seventeen years old, his parents sent him to Indianapolis in search of better educational opportunities. While attending Shortridge High School, he lived at the Senate Avenue YMCA and waited tables to support himself.

He graduated from Shortridge High School in 1921 and attended the University of Illinois on scholarship for two years. He served as the editor of the student newspaper, the *College Dreamer*. Richardson briefly returned to Huntsville because of his mother's death. He moved to Indianapolis in 1925 and earned a Bachelor of Laws degree (LLB) from Indiana Law School in 1928.

He was appointed as temporary judge in Marion County Superior Court in 1930 and was elected to the Indiana House of Representatives on the Democratic ticket in 1932. He sponsored legislation in 1935 to amend the state constitution to allow the integration of the Indiana National Guard and also spearheaded a movement to end discrimination in housing in the dormitories of Indiana University.

In 1947, he chaired a committee that drafted, sponsored, and lobbied to secure passage of Indiana's "Anti-Hate" Law to eliminate racial segregation in the state. In 1949, he worked tirelessly to secure passage of Indiana's school desegregation law and was an outspoken critic of racial prejudice and discrimination. In the 1970s, he was among Indianapolis's African American community leaders who adamantly opposed Mayor Richard Lugar's Uni-Gov legislation, a plan to consolidate some municipal and county government and disenfranchise the African American community. Richardson died on December 5, 1983, in Indianapolis.[21]

The Indianapolis Public Schools produced educators who fought for freedom and equality for African Americans in Indianapolis. Some risked death and the possible loss of employment, but nevertheless fought valiantly. There was one who stepped from the classroom on to the picket line and shone a bright light on inequality in education in Indianapolis. Andrew W. Ramsey (fig. 23.6) was born on November 23, 1905, to Joseph and Leonard Hearod Ramsey in McMinnville, Tennessee. He graduated from Shortridge High School in 1922 and received his bachelor's degree in French from Butler University and his master's degree in French from Indiana University. Early in his professional career, he taught foreign languages at the Louisville Municipal College for Negroes in Louisville,

Fig. 23.6 Andrew Ramsey, educator and civil rights activist. Courtesy of Indiana Historical Society.

Kentucky, which was a segregated institution under the administration of the Board of Trustees of the University of Louisville. It was the only full-fledged Black liberal arts college in Kentucky and the only one in the nation supported by city funds.

He married Sophia Tate-Ramsey and relocated to Indianapolis, where he taught French and Spanish at Crispus Attucks High School. For more than a quarter of a century, the editorial pages of the most prominent African American newspaper in Indianapolis, the *Indianapolis Recorder*, featured a lively column called Voice from the Gallery. From 1946 until his death in 1973, Ramsey, a soft-spoken and urbane African American teacher, wrote for the weekly newspaper's provocative essays, with topics ranging from the commercialization of Christmas to basketball yet remaining united by the consistent themes of African American civil rights and the need to achieve a racially integrated country. In the words of the *Indianapolis Recorder*, Ramsey's essays "battled the many-headed monster of white supremacy" and confronted any "person or institution . . . which sins against the light of human liberty."[22]

Ramsey's experiences as a teacher in Indianapolis's segregated Crispus Attucks High School informed his long-standing efforts to integrate the city's schools. Ramsey's writings reflected the work of an informed, politically active teacher and provide a valuable perspective on the process of school desegregation as it evolved in a northern city.

Ramsey was the president of the local and state chapters of the NAACP, and while teaching at Shortridge High School, he fought racial bias within the Indianapolis Public School System and helped to initiate the lawsuits against the Indianapolis Public School Board that resulted in the desegregation of the school system.

In early 1968, a parent of a public school student filed a complaint with the US Department of Justice about the alleged lack of racial integration within the Indiana Public School System, which violated the US Supreme Court's 1954 decision in *Brown v. Board of Education*. The attorneys of the Justice Department investigated the claims, although action was not immediately taken. According to the *Indianapolis Star*, Ramsey and other NAACP officials conducted a letter-writing campaign to the Justice Department, encouraging action on segregation within Indiana public schools.

On April 27, 1968, the Justice Department filed a notice of intent to sue the Indiana Public School Board. One month later, on May 31, 1968, a lawsuit was filed in the District Court of Indianapolis. This commenced thirteen years of litigation, which also involved the Marion County township schools. Issues relating to the initial lawsuit, especially regarding busing, continued to be litigated into the late 1990s.

Andrew Ramsey retired from teaching in 1972 and died in May 1973. On May 18, 1974, the city dedicated a park in his honor.[23]

The religious community produced heroes who waged war from the pulpit. Many pastors were reluctant to challenge the status quo for fear of reprisal from the majority community, but one gladiator fought fearlessly without concern for his personal safety. Andrew Johnny Brown was born on November 20, 1921, in Duncan, Mississippi, a survivor of a twin birth to a mother who he never knew and father, Amos Brown. He was raised by his maternal grandparents, Forest and Margie Jefferson. He was born a twin, but his sibling did not survive. A few months after his birth, Brown was taken to Indianapolis. According to the 1930 Federal Census, he resided with his grandparents in the western sector of Indianapolis near Indiana Avenue. During his early childhood, his deeply religious grandparents instilled in him a sense of self-worth, Christian hope, and pride in his Black heritage.

In his teenage years, he moved to Chicago and lived with his aunt, Mattie Jefferson Pollard. He attended Ebenezer Missionary Baptist Church and gained recognition as one of the top vocalists in the choir. Later, he transitioned from religious to secular music and performed in programs and venues throughout Chicago. The highlight of his young musical career was realized when he performed with the immensely popular bandleader Cab Calloway and song stylist Dinah Washington. In 1938, he graduated from DuSable High School.

During World War II, he joined the US Army on March 26, 1943. While stationed overseas, he immediately realized that there were very few African American chaplains to serve the spiritual needs of Black soldiers. He sought and received a field commission from General Dwight David Eisenhower and became a chaplain.

According to his obituary, "there were very few Black Chaplains in the United States Army. In World War II, seeing the need for spiritual guidance for Black soldiers, Reverend Brown sought and received a field commission from General D. Eisenhower and became a Chaplain in the United States Army. Later, while serving, he sustained a leg injury. Reverend Brown was shipped to an 'all-white hospital' in Camp Livingston, Louisiana, where he was told his leg would have to be amputated. That Christmas night as Reverend Brown lay on the back porch of this hospital with his leg in traction, he began to redefine his purpose and mission as an evangelist. He prayed to God that if He would save his leg from being amputated, he would devote the remainder of his life preaching the message of salvation for humanity and fighting against social injustice. Around three o'clock that same morning, Reverend Brown clearly recalled the face of a Red Cross nurse who came out to the porch and gave him some apples and oranges. The nurse remembered that he had not received anything for Christmas. The

White soldiers within the hospitals had received gifts. She sadly recounted to him that she had not been able to sleep because of thoughts of the lack of concern shown him by the staff simply because he was Black. She apologized for the Jim Crow Laws. These memories and other social atrocities caused Reverend Brown to continually cry out until he was heard in later years."[24]

Brown attended Bishop College in Marshall, Texas, where civil rights activism was a hot button issue, and became one of the leaders in the struggle. He joined forces with other activist students such as Coleman W. Henry, who was later appointed by President Richard Nixon to the Education Task Force of North Carolina, and George Dudley, who became president of the City Council of Rocky Mountain, North Carolina. Later, he attended the Butler University School of Religion, and he received an honorary Doctor of Divinity degree from the Christian Theological Seminary and delivered the Commencement Address on May 17, 1987.

In 1963, Brown organized the African American community and formed a single voting bloc to demonstrate the power of the Black vote. His parishioners and community activists took the religious zeal and spiritual energy of the civil rights struggle into the arenas of politics, business, government, education, economics, and community development. Reverend Brown and his parishioners also provided leadership and support to the African American community and protested police brutality and unfair hiring practices, staged freedom rallies, and led marches with picket signs.

On many occasions, Dr. Martin Luther King Jr. spoke at activist churches in Indianapolis, and he was conversely condemned by other reluctant churches that feared economic and political reprisals from segments of the Indianapolis majority. In order to ensure his safety, Dr. King was, on numerous occasions, an honored guest at the home of Reverend Brown and family.

In 1968, Reverend Brown took the reins of the Indiana Christian Leadership Conference (ICLC), which was an affiliate of the Southern Christian Leadership Conference. As president of the ICLC, he criticized African Americans for being too complacent and urged them to join the Poor People's March on Washington in May 1968. After the assassination of Dr. Martin Luther King Jr., in April 1968, the ICLC was one of three organizations in the United States to commemorate the birthday of Dr. King, fifteen years before it became a national holiday under the administration of President Ronald Reagan in 1983.

In 1971, Indiana Black Expo was birthed by the ICLC and cosponsored by several African American organizations. Jim Cummings became the first president of the Indiana Black Expo. Reverend Brown, with the assistance of local community organizations, volunteers, and Willard Ransom, a prominent

Indianapolis attorney, secured a $20,000 bank loan to help finance the event. The three-day celebration brought fifty thousand attendees to the Indiana State Fairgrounds and grossed nearly $70,000.

When asked about his visions of tomorrow, Reverend Brown stated introspectively and emphatically: "So once the storms of oppression are ranging upon us, then we'll realize that we Blacks must band together for survival and self-development. We United States Blacks represent the largest group of organized Blacks in the world. We have more capital than any third-world nation. This shows potential. Blacks must keep the faith that has sustained us for so many years. The Black church must maintain its historic centrality for all Black people." Dr. Andrew J. Brown died on August 2, 1996.[25]

"It takes a village to raise a child" is an old Nigerian proverb wherein an esteemed individual of an African village, not necessarily related to a child by blood, has the responsibility of instilling good morals in all children so that they develop great character and high ideals and make the village proud. Perhaps in the Nigerian village the esteemed elder may have been called Mr. Adebayo or Ms. Morenike; however, across the Atlantic Ocean in the African American community of Indianapolis, during the 1950s, the esteemed village elder was called Mr. S. Henry Bundles.

S. Henry Bundles was born on February 15, 1927, as the seventh child of Mary Ellis Davis and S. Henry Bundles Sr. He did not enter this world with the proverbial silver spoon in his mouth. According to his daughter, award-winning author and journalist A'Lelia Bundles, "Long ago he told me that his family was so poor during the depression that they couldn't afford a birthday cake. Instead, his mother made a platter of red Jello for her 'June Bug' [his nickname] written in whipped cream." Bundles attended the segregated Frederick Douglass Elementary School 19 on the far southern side of Indianapolis and graduated from Crispus Attucks High School in 1943, when he was sixteen years old.[26]

In 1944, Bundles enrolled in Indiana University and chose journalism as a major. During the spring semester of 1945, he returned to Indianapolis and played baseball on a couple of semiprofessional teams that barnstormed throughout small towns in Indiana and Kentucky. By mid-August, a few days prior to the V-J (Victory over Japan) Day celebration marking the day the Empire of Japan surrendered to Allied Forces and effectively ended World War II, Bundles reported for duty at the US Naval Base at Great Lakes, near Chicago, Illinois.

He completed boot camp and was assigned to the Naval Aviation Photographic Unit under the command of Lieutenant Commander Edward Steichen. He operated moving picture projectors, worked in the photography laboratory

for the base newspaper, and trained in basic photography, photographic process-
ing, and journalism. His special services indoctrination and training further
prepared him for a career in print media.

A 1948 graduate, he was the first African American student to earn a degree
from the Indiana University School of Journalism. It was a sign of the times that
despite this degree and his experience as a photographer and reporter during
his stint in the US Navy, Indianapolis daily newspapers would not hire him in
an editorial position, assumably because of the color of his skin. Undeterred,
he became a circulation manager at the *Indianapolis News* daily newspaper and
learned the business side of journalism while he mentored and managed young
Crispus Attucks/Indiana Avenue–area students who delivered newspapers.

Many of the paper delivery boys were from impoverished households from
the west side neighborhoods of Indianapolis. They delivered the *Indianapolis
Star* or the *Indianapolis News* daily newspapers, and in many instances their
earnings helped put food on their tables. Bundles recognized this fact and made
sure that these youngsters were equipped with proper business knowledge and
operational procedures that would empower them to succeed in the business
world. He taught them how to manage their savings accounts and conduct themselves in a professional business manner. One youngster, Hallie Bryant—who
was a basketball star at Crispus Attucks High School in 1953, became Mr. Basketball (an honor that denoted the most outstanding high school basketball
player in the state of Indiana), and later starred at Indiana University and then
the world-famous Harlem Globetrotters—fondly remembers how Bundles impacted his life: "He helped when he could and hindered none. He tried to teach
us honesty . . . to be on time . . . and to tell the truth . . . and be the best person
that you could possibly be."[27]

According to another newspaper carrier, John Dumas-Haamid:

> Mr. Bundles was like a father figure to some of the youngsters who didn't
> have fathers in their home, as an adult and operating my barbershop, one
> period I was on hard times and financially unable to buy my products to
> operate my barbershop, I went to Mr. Bundles and told him about my
> dilemma and asked him if I could pay him on time. He told me empathi-
> cally, "No!" He told me to go into his warehouse, take all what I needed to
> get back on my feet and not to worry about paying him back. That was Mr.
> Bundles! He was an astute businessman, highly educated and all but un-
> like many corporate giants of today, he cared about the downtrodden and
> had a heart of gold.[28]

Bundles married A'Lelia Mae Perry Bundles in June 1950, and a few years
later he became sales and advertising manager for the Madam C. J. Walker

Fig. 23.8 S. Henry Bundles, founder of the Center for Leadership Development. Courtesy of A'Lelia Bundles.

Manufacturing Company, the firm founded by his wife's great-grandmother. He was successful at sales and business development and was hired as president and chief operations officer of Summit Laboratories, an international hair-care-products company that he led to regular rankings on the *Black Enterprise* 100. In addition to accomplishing great things in the business world, he broke barriers on many boards and organizations, serving as a director of the Indianapolis

Convention and Visitors Association, a founding director of Midwest National Bank, and chairman of the Indianapolis Business Development Foundation. He immensely enjoyed being an Indianapolis 500 Festival director as much for the leadership opportunities as for the perk of driving one of the thirty-three limited-edition convertible pace cars.[29]

In 1976, after the death of his wife, Bundles (fig. 23.8) launched the Center for Leadership Development, an organization designed to prepare youth of color to become professional business and community leaders. When he retired in 2000, he and his team had mentored more than two thousand students annually. It is a testament to the institution that he helped build that the Center for Leadership Development awarded more than $5 million in scholarships at its annual Minority Achievers Awards and Scholarship Gala. In addition, three generations of Center for Leadership Development alumni hold leadership positions throughout the world in medicine, law, education, finance, media, ministry, and other professions. They all remembered the mantra that Bundles quoted at the beginning of each session: "In Time. On Time. Every Time. Except when ahead of time, and that's better time."[30]

At one speaking engagement a few days after her father died, A'Lelia Bundles reminisced, "It no longer surprises me when I'm making a speech and someone in the audience comes up to let me know that they're a graduate of the Center for Leadership Development. In fact, last week at Vorhees College, Demark South Carolina, Gwynth R. Nelson, the school's Vice President for Institutional Advancement and Development, introduced herself as a proud Center for Leadership Development alumna."[31]

S. Henry Bundles dedicated his life to the uplift and betterment of his community in Indianapolis. He treated everyone, whether a prince or a pauper, with the same degree of respect and loyalty. His mission in life was to empower youth so they could enjoy success in life and be trailblazers in their communities. The youth of Indianapolis were fortunate to have such a wonderful village elder walking among them. S. Henry Bundles died on March 26, 2017.

TWENTY-FOUR

—ᴥ—

WOMEN OF VALOR

THE STRUGGLE TOWARD FREEDOM AND equality in Indianapolis highlighted the courageous exploits of men of color, who surmounted incredible barriers in an uncompromising and racist society. Although these men's names were featured in the headlines of newspapers period and they enjoyed overwhelming praise from the community, there were numerous African American women who made outstanding contributions that were not celebrated and, in some cases, were completely ignored. However, if not for the determination and perseverance of these women, many of the gains made during the two centuries of the history of Indianapolis would have been impossible.

Mary Ellen Montgomery Cable was born in 1862 in Leavenworth, Kansas. She graduated from Leavenworth High School and Teacher's Normal College and later became a teacher in the Topeka (Kansas) Public School System. While in Topeka, she married George W. Cable, and they relocated to Indianapolis in 1893. Her husband gained employment with the US Post Office, and Cable began a forty-year career with the Indianapolis Public School System. In the early twentieth century, she supervised the African American Community Elementary School Vegetable Garden Project. This initiative was designed to plant gardens and to beautify neighborhoods in the community.

Later, during the school years of 1916–1917, she established the first fresh-air program at Public School 4 for students infected with tuberculosis. She held many positions, including teacher, principal, director, and supervisor of teachers. She trained sixty-one teachers who became outstanding teachers and principals and five of whom became outstanding educators and principals. Cable retired in 1933, after a remarkable career in education and community service. She was a member of Bethel AME Church and the Sigma Gamma Rho sorority and was the first president of the Indianapolis branch of the NAACP. May Ellen Montgomery Cable died on September 18, 1944.

Harriette Bailey Conn was a warrior. She was a political pioneer and mighty force who worked tirelessly to improve the quality of life in her community. She struggled against seemingly insurmountable odds to become a distinguished attorney and public servant dedicated to the advancement of her people in every aspect of the Indianapolis community.

Harriet Bailey Conn (fig. 24.1) was born on September 22, 1922, to Robert L. Bailey and Nelle Vesta Bailey in Indianapolis, Indiana. Her father, a prominent civil rights attorney, served as an Indiana deputy attorney general from 1930 to 1932. He was actively involved with the NAACP. She graduated from Crispus Attucks High School in 1937 and then attended Talladega College in Talladega, Alabama, where she majored in English and speech. In 1955, she graduated from the Indiana University School of Law. She served as a deputy attorney general the following year, and she worked with the Indiana Civil Rights Commission, the Indiana State Teachers' Retirement Fund, the Indiana Public Employees Retirement Fund, and the Indiana State Highway Department.

Conn served two terms in the Indiana State Legislature. In 1968, she served as assistant city attorney in the Richard Lugar administration. Harriette Bailey Conn died on August 21, 1981, in Indianapolis.[1]

Indianapolis was fortunate to have a powerful leader in the community who dedicated her life to neighborhood preservation. Mattie Rice Coney realized that a beautiful, well-maintained community gave residents a sense of pride and appreciation in their neighborhood, which translated into positive personal relationships among residents.

Mattie Rice Coney was born on May 30, 1909, to Salon and Delia Porter-House in Gallatin, Tennessee. When she was six weeks old, her family relocated to Indianapolis, whereupon her parents divorced. Her mother, a cook, married Oscar Weathers, and the family resided near Indiana Avenue. Her mother's family members were industrious and entrepreneurial-minded individuals. An uncle owned a milk business, and two relatives operated stands in the city market in downtown Indianapolis. Other relatives operated a successful barbershop and the largest hot tamale business in town. From her family members, she gained the motivation to obtain a good education, to strive toward excellence in her community, and to value the importance of perseverance, hard work, and self-reliance.

Coney was a product of the Indianapolis Public School System and graduated from Shortridge High School in 1927. She financed her education at Butler University by delivering newspapers and working as a waitress at the L. S. Ayres

Fig. 24.1 Harriette Bailey Conn, attorney and civil rights activist. Courtesy of
J. Sidney Conn.

and Company's Tearoom. She continued her education at Indiana State University, Western Reserve University, and Columbia University.

She was passionately concerned with the deterioration of many inner-city African American communities and took drastic steps to remedy the problem. In 1964, she and her husband, Elmo, were the driving forces behind the Citizens Forum, an organization of various community improvement associations that fought for the elimination of neighborhood blight, for a city beautification program, and for streets safe for school children.

Her philosophy empowered the community to incorporate self-reliance and introspection in their daily neighborhood activities. She believed that city government should not be solely responsible for the maintenance of neighborhoods and that citizens had the power and responsibility to solve their problems by working cohesively and collaboratively with other community groups throughout the city.

She received accolades from all segments of the community in reference to her remarkable contributions in neighborhood preservation, but the crowning point of her career was receiving a letter from a former president of the United States. Dwight D. Eisenhower had learned of her efforts to better the community's neighborhoods and took the time to write a personal letter. "Not only have I been impressed by our common sense philosophy," he wrote, "but even more by the patriotism, energy, and organizing ability that are so evident in the record you have made."

She was respected nationally, and her articles were published in the *US News and World Report* and the *New York Times*. She was popular and respected locally, and she received honorary degrees from Butler University, the University of Indianapolis, and Hillsdale College in Hillsdale, Michigan. Mattie Rice Coney died on August 5, 1988, in Indianapolis.[2]

From humble beginnings, one individual triumphed against all odds and made her community better. She was not born with the proverbial silver spoon in her mouth. As a matter of fact, she was not blessed with a spoon but with painful memories of abject poverty. Early in Julia May Carson's life, she learned the virtue of compassion when she was a youngster whose family was in need of help. She arrived at an Indianapolis Welfare Office seeking assistance to feed her family and was treated with so much contempt and disrespect that she felt completely humiliated. She left the office in tears. This event galvanized her determination to help the poor as she recognized the vulnerability of citizens of all colors who were in need. She spent her entire life as a champion of the poor and downtrodden.

Julia May Carson (fig. 24.2) was born on December 15, 1938, to a young unmarried Velma V. Porter in Louisville, Kentucky. Her father was absent

Fig. 24.2 Julia Carson, the first African American to represent Indiana in the US Congress. Courtesy of Crispus Attucks Museum, Indianapolis Public Schools.

throughout her life. Her mother relocated to Indianapolis during Julia's early years and worked as a domestic worker to support her family. Julia helped her mother economically and worked as a waitress, newspaper girl, and migrant farmer. She attended the Indianapolis Public School System and graduated from Crispus Attucks High School in 1955.

She married after graduation, had two children, and divorced during the children's early years. Later, she attended Martin University and Indiana University–Purdue University at Indianapolis. In 1965, she worked as a secretary at the United Auto Workers Local 550, and she left this position to work for newly elected congressman Andrew Jacobs Jr. as a caseworker in his Indianapolis office.

In 1972, Carson, with the encouragement of Jacobs, ran for a seat in the Indiana House of Representatives and won. She served as a delegate for four years and became assistant minority caucus chair. Later, she ran for the Indiana Senate and won and served there for fourteen years. Carson and Katie Hall of Lake County became the first African American women to win seats in the Indiana Senate.

In 1990, Carson triumphed in the election of the trustee for Center Township, and she served for six years. During her term, her administration focused on austerity, fiscal and responsibility, eliminating a $20 million deficit and created a $6 million surplus.

In 1996, when Andy Jacobs retired from the Tenth Congressional District, Carson ran against Republican Virginia Blankenbaker and won. During her distinguished tenure, Carson introduced legislation to award civil rights icon Rosa Parks with the Congressional Gold Medal and cosponsored with Senator Richard Lugar the removal of bureaucratic bottlenecks on child health insurance. For Indianapolis, Carson secured federal funding to revitalize the Fall Creek neighborhood and to construct the Indianapolis International Airport. Julia May Carson died on December 15, 2007.[3]

Equality and integration in education was the hallmark of one women's contribution to the Indianapolis community. On relocating to Indianapolis, Roselyn Richardson immediately recognized that every Indianapolis child should have the opportunity to obtain a quality education. She battled gallantly against public school segregation. Assisted with the agency of neighborhood, religious, and educational organizations, she took on the task to level the playing field in public education. She received much criticism from the majority community in her march toward justice, but she continued her battle with integrity, dignity and respect.

Rosalyn Comer Richardson was born on August 23, 1913, to Arthur and Everlena Comer in Roberta, Georgia. Her family encouraged her to take her education seriously so she could succeed in life. She attended a Spartanly equipped, one-room Black country school that terminated at the fifth grade. Afterward, she studied privately, and at fourteen years of age, she entered a boarding school for Blacks run by the Episcopal Church in Fort Valley, Georgia. She attended Fort Valley Industrial High School in 1930 and later graduated from Clark College in Atlanta, Georgia. Two years later, she received her master's degree in community organization and group work from the School of Social Work at Atlanta University. In 1938, she married the prominent attorney Henry J. Richardson.

Initially after relocating to Indianapolis, Richardson obtained membership in female organizations dedicated to progressive ideas. One of the organizations was the YWCA, an interracial group of professional women. She immediately became disenchanted with the attitudes of several women: "The Young

Women's Christian Association sponsored one interracial group, but the meetings between white women who acted like they were doing you a favor by coming and Black women who acted like they [were] less than stimulating."[4]

In 1946, Richardson attempted to enroll her son in an Indianapolis public school a few blocks from her home. "Our neighborhood was changing and the school was half empty. But the catch was that it was all white," she recounted.[5] The school administrators rejected her admission application and advised her to transport her son to a "colored school" two miles from her home. Infuriated by the rebuff, Richardson swung into action and began a movement that would change Indianapolis history.

Exasperated, Richardson spearheaded a campaign to travel around the city and make residents aware of the inequality and racism exhibited by the Indianapolis Public School System. "We called neighborhood meetings and started running around town organizing black people." She canvassed grocery stores, beauty shops, bridge clubs, and other social gatherings to spread the message. She later received support from the Unitarian and Jewish communities, and political momentum was in her favor.

The National NAACP joined the movement and sent Thurgood Marshall to Indianapolis to coordinate a potential test case. Richardson and other Black Indianapolis civic leaders met with Governor Henry F. Schricker to discuss a resolution to the racial problem that would not consume too much time. Motivated by Richardson's courage and insight, a desegregation bill was drafted. "Mom was a superior community organizer and dad took care of the legislature, drafting legislation," related Henry Richardson III.[6] On March 8, 1949, the bill ostensibly ended segregation in all Indiana public schools. Rosalyn Comer Richardson sparked a movement that changed Indiana public education forever. She was also instrumental in the establishment of the Indianapolis Urban League, served on the board of the Phyllis Wheatley YWCA, and served as director of the Flanner Guild. Roselyn Comer Richardson died on July 8, 2005.[7]

During the middle of the twentieth century, with the issues of public schools and college segregation, bus boycotts, sit-ins, and civil rights marches, Indianapolis had a really tough fighter who worked hard for equality and took no prisoners. Osma Duffus Spurlock (fig. 24.4) was born on December 27, 1917, to Harold and Louise Duffus in Charleston, South Carolina, and was raised in New York City. She received a Bachelor of Science degree from Hunter College in New York City and a Master of Science degree from Atlanta University. In 1988, she received an honorary doctorate from Martin University in Indianapolis. She began her career with the Flanner House, where she worked with Dr. Cleo Blackburn in the development of a home construction program. It was one

Fig. 24.3 Osma Duffus Spurlock, deputy director of the Indiana Civil Rights Commission. Courtesy of Anita Gordon.

of the first community projects in the United States designed to build homes for African Americans that employed labor as equity for a first down payment. She was the first deputy director of the Indiana Civil Rights Commission. She was first woman and African American director of the Indianapolis Office of the Equal Employment Opportunity Commission.

Her community commitment was expansive, and she was a member of the National Board of the Girl Scouts of America, the Indianapolis Chapter of the National Urban League, and the 100 Black Women of Indianapolis. She received the Indiana Civil Rights Spirit of Justice Award. Osma Duffus Spurlock died on April 18, 2007, in Indianapolis.[8]

The Indianapolis community was blessed to have these dynamic women who blazed trails for other citizens to follow. Although they often worked in the shadows and did not receive the recognition of their male counterparts, they nevertheless made outstanding contributions to the city and state, contributions that made Indianapolis a more hospitable city in which to live. Future generations will glance backwards to these important episodes in Indianapolis history and realize the great advancements that were achieved by these mighty warriors.

TWENTY-FIVE

URBAN RENEWAL IS NEGRO REMOVAL

THE ASSASSINATIONS OF THE KENNEDYS, Malcolm X, and Dr. Martin Luther King Jr. College campuses erupting in protest of an increasingly unpopular war in Vietnam. The deaths of college students from Kent State University and South Carolina State College by jittery National Guardsmen. The cries of "Black Power" by civil rights activists Stokely Carmichael and H. Rap Brown. The phenomena of the 1960s reverberated from Los Angeles to Newark, New Jersey.

In Indianapolis, these events ignited social unrest and outrage that still simmer in the African American community today. African Americans glanced back over the sixth decade of the twentieth century to evaluate and enumerate social, political, and economic gains. Had the dreams and aspirations envisioned at the onset of the century been realized? How much farther must we travel to become bona fide citizens of Indianapolis? What challenges down the road might block African American progress? What tools should we employ to protect social, economic, and political gains already achieved?

At the onset of the seventh decade, several significant events made the celebration of past achievements moot.

In 1969, under the leadership of Mayor Richard Lugar, the first salvo was launched at the African American community when a plan called Uni-Gov was devised, introduced, and implemented. Under this plan, the executive and legislative bodies of Indianapolis and Marion County were consolidated to create a single, strong council with a single county-wide executive. The voting power of African Americans was drastically weakened when a quarter of a million white constituents were added to the voting rolls. In 1968, almost 90 percent of African Americans lived in Center Township of Marion County, and 25 percent of the voting base was Black. After the introduction of Uni-Gov, the African American vote plunged to 18 percent.[1] Outrage was anticipated.

Indianapolis's Black community, particularly along Indiana Avenue, had been displaced in the 1960s with the establishment of IUPUI and the interstate. The health and influence of the cleaved Black community would again be diminished with the passage of Uni-Gov. Many people feared—and history bore this out—that the new voters and the predominately white council would act in their own best interests, prioritizing skyscrapers over, for example, struggling public schools. Some also worried that Uni-Gov's planners sought to eliminate the possibility of a Black mayor.[2]

There was an immediate outcry in the African American community. Willard Ransom, a prominent Indianapolis attorney and head of the NAACP registered his outrage. He stated, "Lugar brought the worst curse on all of us . . . Uni-Gov. We fought him on that but he got it through. That brought the outlying areas of the city to vote. Uni-Gov was the big thing that Lugar did that was bad for blacks."[3] The apparent disenfranchisement of the Black community resulted in serious repercussions. Many felt that they had been hoodwinked by the Republican Party in an effort to seize political power. Also, they felt that the nationally publicized elections of African Americans Carl Stokes of Cleveland and Richard Hatcher of Gary, Indiana, as mayors in their respective cities proved to be a bad omen for Republicans, who perhaps surmised, "Could this happen here . . . a black mayor in Indianapolis?"[4]

The second salvo launched by the federal government and the city administration was the construction of Interstate 65. This project disrupted the racial, cultural, historical, and architectural integrity of Indiana Avenue and the surrounding communities. African American communities were torn to shreds, and as a result, many lifelong homeowners and tenants were forced from their residences to seek refuge in the corners of the city. In spite of protests from the Congress of Racial Equality (CORE), the project prevailed, and the Indiana Avenue community and its entertainment complex were decimated.[5]

The third salvo launched toward the African American community arrived in 1968, with the expansion of Indiana University in partnership with Purdue University. The catalyst of this project was once again Mayor Richard Lugar, who longed for the establishment of a great state university in Indianapolis.

Throughout much of the 1960s, as reforming activists within the Republican Party met to plot their strategies, one of their ultimate goals was an independent state university in Indianapolis. Successful in their immediate goal of wrestling control of the Marion County Republican Party from the ineffective leadership of county chairman H. Dale Brown in 1966, they turned at once to the issue of higher education and made plans to introduce legislation, once all the necessary offices had been filled in the election of 1968, that would create the long-desired independent state university in Indianapolis.

Near the campus was the Lockefield Garden public housing development, which had been constructed in 1938 under President Franklin Delano Roosevelt's New Deal program. It was built for low-income African Americans, many of whom were veterans from World War I or residents who had previously resided in substandard, dilapidated housing. It covered twenty-two acres and had twenty-four buildings with 748 units. Many African American families took great pride in maintaining its beauty and made great efforts to ensure its upkeep and vitality. Later there were families who struggled to improve their circumstances in life and who overcame poverty and became role models for other upwardly mobile families. Slowly but surely, these determined families who found better employment and earned more money were required to vacate their apartments in accordance with the rental policy of the Indianapolis Housing Authority. Consequently, the families who replaced them were more impoverished, and, as a result, the social landscape changed. Many apartments were vacant, there was refuse in the yards, and a serious drug distribution problem developed. The beautiful, pristine Lockefield Gardens public housing development of earlier decades was gone forever.

Ultimately, Indiana University–Purdue University at Indianapolis (IUPUI) took control of the project, and many families had to vacate Lockefield Gardens and the Indiana Avenue area. More than five thousand families were forced to move from their ancestral downtown neighborhood without city or federal financial assistance. The regulation of eminent domain forced the residents, and they had no legal recourse to save their neighborhood. Indiana Avenue history and culture were extinguished.

With the fourth salvo successfully launched toward the African American community, a sense of general malaise, outrage, and disillusionment permeated the atmosphere. Then it happened. In June 1969, the Indianapolis Police Department was summoned to Lockefield Gardens to investigate a domestic disturbance. The two Caucasian officers dispatched were informed by Richard Ellis that their services were not needed and that local community leaders could resolve the dispute. The officers responded by drawing their guns. Suddenly, Richard Earl Ellis, a young African American man, grabbed the gun of one of the officers and ran into the housing development where children played. The

Fig. 25.1 Albert Coleman, the last African-American entertainment business owner on Indiana Avenue, fought for the area's survival. Courtesy of Albert Coleman.

other officer fired at Ellis and barely missed the youngsters. Residents, angered by the officer's disregard for human life, stormed onto Indiana Avenue and rioted and burned businesses.[6]

In the aftermath of these four salvos and resultant riot, white and Black businesses left Indiana Avenue in fear of future riots and destruction. Many of the entertainment venues closed. Longtime, devoted patrons of Indiana Avenue vacated the area and vowed never to return. The last entertainment venue to shut its doors was Al Coleman's British Lounge (fig. 25.1). Indiana Avenue entertainment died a painful death, and its torch of hope and prosperity was extinguished forever.[7] Albert Coleman reflected further on the closing of Indiana Avenue: "I didn't feel too good about it, because the Avenue was a place where we could go and enjoy ourselves and we had top line entertainment and big bands like Duke Ellington and Count Basie. I knew they were trying to close the Avenue down. They offered me two relocation properties. One at the Union Station and the other behind the Convention Center. I couldn't have made a go of it at any of these places."[8]

NOTES

1. INDIANA BECOMES A STATE

1. Emma Lou Thornbrough, *The Negro in Indiana before 1900: A Study of a Minority* (Bloomington: Indiana University Press, 1993), 25–30.

2. Logan Esarey, *History of Indiana from Its Exploration to 1922* (Dayton, OH: Dayton Historical Publishing, 1924), 20–25.

3. Joseph Henry VanderBurgh Somes, *Old Vincennes: The History of a Famous Old Town and Its Glorious Past* (New York: Graphic Books, 1962), 44.

4. Thornbrough, *Negro in Indiana*, 24–25.

5. Jacob Piatt Dunn, *Indiana: A Redemption from Slavery* (Boston: Houghton Mifflin, 1905), 220, 224, 226.

6. Eunice Brewer-Trotter, interview by author, July 4, 2020; Eunice Brewer-Trotter, "Mary Bateman Clark: A Woman of Color and Courage," *Traces of Indiana and Midwestern History* 27, no. 4 (Fall 2015): 38.

7. Thornbrough, *Negro in Indiana*, 23–25.

8. Thornbrough, *Negro in Indiana*, 25–30.

9. Thornbrough, *Negro in Indiana*, 52–53.

10. Thornbrough, *Negro in Indiana*, 233–35; Charles Kettleborough, "Constitution Making in Indiana: A Source Book of Constitutional Documents with Historical Introduction and Critical Notes (Vol. I, 1780–1851)," *Journal of American History* 4, no. 2 (September 1917): 260–61.

2. EARLY INDIANAPOLIS

1. Jacob Piatt, *Greater Indianapolis: The History, the Industries, the Institutions and the People of a City of Homes* (Chicago: Lewis, 1930), 8.

2. Piatt, *Greater Indianapolis*.

3. Luther Hicks, *Great Black Hoosier Americans* (Indianapolis: Luther Hicks, 1977), 56–57.

4. Ashley Petry, *Indianapolis: A Guide to the Weird, Wonderful, and Obscure* (St. Louis, MO: Reedy Press, 2019), 124.

5. "Early Gangs Plagued Town," *Indianapolis Star,* November 7, 1971.

6. "Old Dave Burkhardt," *Indianapolis News,* August 18, 1944.

3. THE SHAME OF INDIANAPOLIS

1. *New York Times,* July 16, 1845.

2. Emma Lou Thornbrough, *The Negro in Indiana before 1900: A Study of a Minority* (Bloomington: Indiana University Press, 1993), 129–30.

3. Anton Scherrer, "Our Town," *Indianapolis Times,* July 4, 1936.

4. *Topeka Daily Capital* [Topeka, Kansas], May 8, 1910.

5. Stacey Nicholas, "Freeman, John, Fugitive Slave Case of 1853," in *Encyclopedia of Indianapolis,* ed. David Bodenhamer and Robert G. Barrows (Bloomington: Indiana University Press, 1994), 601–2.

4. LIFE, LIBERTY, AND THE PURSUIT OF HAPPINESS

1. Pamela R. Peters, *The Underground Railroad in Floyd County, Indiana* (Jefferson, NC: McFarland, 2001), 32.

2. Peters, *Underground Railroad,* 83.

3. Emma Lou Thornbrough, *The Negro in Indiana: A Study of a Minority* (Bloomington: Indiana University Press, 1993), 64.

4. Peters, *Underground Railroad,* 11, 12.

5. Peters, *Underground Railroad,* 11, 13.

6. Indiana State Constitution, article 13, section one.

5. "NEGROES, YAW GO BACK TO AFRICA!"

1. Emma Lou Thornbrough, *The Negro in Indiana before 1900: A Study of a Minority* (Bloomington: Indiana University Press, 1993), 141.

2. Thornbrough, *Negro in Indiana,* 146; Stephen Miller, letter to Joseph and Nancy Brown, January 23, 1863, Stephen Miller Collection, Indiana Division, Indiana State Library.

3. Robert J. Price to D. Price, June 6, 1863, Robert J. Price Collection, Indiana History Bureau, Indiana Division, Indiana State Library; *Corydon Indiana Gazette,* February 10, 1820, extracts from Corydon Newspapers, 1820–1838, Indiana State Library.

4. Ousmane K. Power-Greene, *Against the Wind and Tide: The African-American Struggle against the Colonization Movement* (New York: New York University Press, 2014), 103.

5. *Corydon Indiana Gazette,* February 10, 1820.

6. Dorothy Thornbrough and Gayle Riker, *Readings in Indiana History* (Indianapolis: Indiana Historical Bureau, 1956).

7. Walter Edgerton, *A History of Separation in Indiana Yearly Meeting of Friends* (Cincinnati: Achilles Pugh, 1856), 34.

8. Dorothy Thornbrough and Gayle Riker, *Eleventh Annual Report of the Indiana Colonization Society* (Indianapolis: Indiana Historical Bureau, 1975), 469–70.

9. "How the Methodist Church Split in the 1840s," *South Carolina United Methodist Advocate*, January 2013.

10. Thornbrough, *Negro in Indiana*, 68.

11. Pamela R. Peters, *The Underground Railroad in Floyd County, Indiana* (Jefferson, NC: MacFarland, 2001), 11–12.

12. *Report of Reverend John McKay, Circular to Friends of African Colonization*, April 17, 1855, Indiana Division, Indiana State Library.

13. *Diary of Calvin Fletcher*, vol. 4, *1848–1852* (Indianapolis: Indiana Historical Society, 1975).

14. Minutes of the State Board of Colonization, January 10, 1857, Secretary of State Journal, Archives Division, Indiana Historical Bureau.

15. Indiana Emigrants to Liberia, *Indiana Historian*, Indiana Historical Bureau, March 2000, 15–16.

16. Webster-Ashburton Treaty, 1842, Office of the Historian, Foreign Service Institute, US Department of State.

6. THE CIVIL WAR YEARS AND BEYOND

1. Emma Lou Thornbrough, *The Negro in Indiana before 1900: A Study of a Minority* (Bloomington: Indiana University Press, 1993), 183.

2. Thornbrough, *Negro in Indiana*.

3. Thornbrough, *Negro in Indiana*, 173.

4. Thornbrough, *Negro in Indiana*, 173, 177.

5. Thornbrough, *Negro in Indiana*, 196.

6. Chris Sims, "Retro Indy: Civil War Regiment Fought at Crater," *Indianapolis Star*, February 18, 1915.

7. Thornbrough, *Negro in Indiana*, 193–204.

8. Stephen Miller, letter to Joseph and Nancy Brown, January 23, 1863, Stephen Miller Collection, Indiana Division, Indiana State Library.

7. POST–CIVIL WAR ACHIEVEMENT

1. Eunice Brewer-Trotter, "Mary Bateman-Clark: Woman of Courage," *Traces of Indiana and Midwestern History* 27, no. 4 (Fall 2015); Eunice Brewer-Trotter, interview by author, June 16, 2020.

2. Obituary of Hortense Bowman-Howard, *Indianapolis Recorder*, March 6, 1976.

3. *Indianapolis Freeman*, July 1, 1893.

4. Emma Lou Thornbrough, *The Negro in Indiana before 1900: A Study of a Minority* (Bloomington: Indiana University Press, 1993), 323–29.

5. Steven R. Barnett, *Writing Her Story*, Indiana Commission for Women, Indiana Historical Society, Indiana Historical Bureau.

6. Andrew Ritchie, *Major Taylor: The Fastest Bicycle Rider in the World* (San Francisco: Van Der Plas, 1988), 13–34.

8. POWER OF THE FOURTH ESTATE

1. Edward R. Murrow, Radio Television News Directors Association Convention, Chicago, October 15, 1958.

2. Emma Lou Thornbrough, *The Negro in Indiana before 1900: A Study of a Minority* (Bloomington: Indiana University Press, 1993), 334–84.

3. "Gideon's Minstrel Carnival," *Indianapolis Journal*, February 27, 1901.

4. *Indianapolis Colored World*, January 20, 1901, April 30, 1901.

5. *Indianapolis Recorder*, May 17, 1902.

6. *Indianapolis Recorder*, May 27, 1904.

7. "Indianapolis News, a Social Necessity, Henry Hart and His Family of Musicians Always in Demand," *Indianapolis Colored World*, December 5, 1896.

8. Minutes of the Board of Commissioners, Indianapolis Public Schools, September 21, 1935.

9. THE TWENTIETH CENTURY: GOING "UP SOUTH"

1. David Leander Williams, *Indianapolis Jazz: The Masters, Legends and Legacy of Indiana Avenue* (Charleston, SC: History Press, 2014), 21.

2. *Indianapolis Freeman*, February 23, 1918.

3. *Indianapolis Freeman*, January 31, 1920.

10. FRANCIS "FRANK" FLANNER

1. Bruce Buchanan, Flanner and Buchanan family archives, February 24, 2020.

2. Buchanan, family archives, February 24, 2020.

11. WHITE POLICEMEN MURDERED! WHERE'S JESSE COE?

1. William Lynwood Montell, *The Saga of Coe Ridge: A Study in Oral History* (New York: Harper & Row, 1970), 144–51.

2. *Indianapolis Sun*, August 27, 1908.

3. *Indianapolis Sun*, August 29, 1908.

4. *Indianapolis Sun*, August 29, 1908.

12. MADAM C. J. WALKER AND EARLY AFRICAN AMERICAN FEMALE TRAILBLAZERS

1. Malcolm X, speech to Student Non-Violent Coordinating Committee, Selma, Alabama, February 4, 1965.

2. Douglass, Frederick, *The Life and Times of Frederick Douglass: From 1817–1882*, ed. John Lobb (London: Christian Age Office, 1882).

3. Earline Rae Ferguson, "African-Americans Women's Club Work: A Community Affair" (PhD diss., Indiana University, 1997), 19.

4. Ferguson, "African-American Women's Club."

5. A'Lelia Perry Bundles, *Madam C. J. Walker, Entrepreneur* (New York: Chelsea House, 1991), 19, 36.

6. A'Lelia Perry Bundles, *On Her Own Ground: The Life and Times of Madam C. J. Walker* (New York: Scribner, 2001), 161.

7. Bundles, *Madam C. J. Walker, Entrepreneur*, 48, 49.

8. *Indianapolis Recorder*, December 26, 1927.

9. *Indianapolis Recorder*, December 24, 1927.

10. Bob Eagle and Eric S. LeBlanc. *Blues: A Regional Experience* (Santa Barbara, CA: Praeger, 2013), 239–40.

11. David Leander Williams, *Indianapolis Jazz: The Masters, Legends and Legacy of Indiana Avenue* (Charleston, SC: History Press, 2014), 33–34, 47.

13. THE *INDIANAPOLIS RECORDER*, CATALYST FOR CHANGE, AND THE MONSTER MEETINGS AT THE SENATE AVENUE YMCA

1. Emma Lou Thornbrough, *The Negro in Indiana before 1900: A Study of a Minority* (Bloomington: Indiana University Press, 1993), 380–81.

2. Bertram Gardner, "The Negro Men's Christian Association in the Indianapolis Community," Monster Meetings, People Is Our Business, Senate Avenue YMCA, 1950.

3. Robert W. Starms, *Achieving Christian Goals through the Public Forum: An Interpretative Study of the Monster Meeting* (Indianapolis: Senate Avenue YMCA, 1944), 6.

4. Starms, *Achieving Christian Goals*.

14. THE ROARIN' TWENTIES

1. Olivia Waxman, "'It's a Struggle They Will Wage Alone': How Black Women Won the Right to Vote," *Time*, August 14, 2020.

2. Robert W. Starms, *Achieving Christian Social Goals through the Public Forum: An Interpretative Study of the Monster Meeting* (Indianapolis: Senate Avenue YMCA, 1944).

3. M. William Lutholtz, *Grand Dragon: D. C. Stephenson and the Ku Klux Klan in Indiana* (West Lafayette, IN: Purdue University Press, 1993), 8–15.

4. Madgelyn Hawk, *When the Mourning Dove Cries* (self-published, Authorhouse, 2003), 131–48.

15. DAVID CURTIS STEPHENSON AND THE KU KLUX KLAN

1. John Kaplan, Robert Weisberg, and Guyora Binder, *Criminal Law: Cases and Materials*, 7th ed. (New York: Wolters Kluwer Law and Business, 2012);

interview with Dr. John Morton-Finney, *Attucks: The School That Opened a City* (documentary file, dir. Ted Green; Ted Green films, 2016).

2. M. William Lutholtz, *Grand Dragon: D. C. Stephenson and the Ku Klux Klan in Indiana* (West Lafayette, IN: Purdue University Press, 1993), 44–46.

3. Lutholtz, *Grand Dragon*, 184–87.

4. Lutholtz, *Grand Dragon*, 192–96.

5. H. R. Greenapple, *D. C. Stephenson Irvington 0492: The Demise of the Grand Dragon of the Indiana Ku Klux Klan* (Plainfield, IN: SGS, 1989), 3–16.

16. CRISPUS ATTUCKS HIGH SCHOOL: "MIRACLE IN THE GHETTO"

1. Booker T. Washington, *Up from Slavery: An Autobiography* (New York: Double Day, 1901), 3–16.

2. Shortridge High School Collection, 1870, 1981, 1995, Indiana Historical Society, January 2002, 1.

3. Stanley Warren, *Crispus Attucks High School: Hail to the Green, Hail to the Gold* (Virginia Beach, VA: Donning, 1998), 47–48.

4. John Morton-Finney Papers, *Black History News and Notes*, February 2005, 15, 20, 80–81.

5. "New Greathouse Hearing," *Indianapolis Recorder*, June 19, 1926.

6. Warren, *Crispus Attucks High School*, 31, 32.

7. Warren, *Crispus Attucks High School*, 34, 35.

8. Warren, *Crispus Attucks High School*, 32–34; Noble Nolcox, interview with Ted Green, *Attucks: The School That Opened a City* (documentary file, dir. Ted Green; Ted Green films, 2016).

9. Warren, *Crispus Attucks High School*, 80, 81.

17. A DECADE OF TURMOIL: LOCKEFIELD GARDENS

1. Roberta Senechal de la Roche, *The Springfield Riot of 1908: Lincoln's Shadow* (Carbondale: Southern Illinois Press, 1990), 10.

2. Allison Keyes, "The East St. Louis Race Riot Left Dozens Dead, Devastating a Community on the Rise," *Smithsonian Magazine*, June 30, 2017.

3. "Scottsboro Boys," *Indianapolis Recorder*, July 31, 1937.

4. "Ethiopian Invasion," *Indianapolis Recorder*, May 9, 1936.

5. "Jesse Owens," *Jewish Post*, August 14, 1936.

6. Pickens, *Indianapolis Recorder*, July 7, 1938.

7. David J. Bodenhamer and Robert G. Barrows, *The Encyclopedia of Indianapolis* (Bloomington: Indiana University Press, 1994), 926–27.

8. Leslie Martin, interview, February 13, 2019.

18. HEROES OF WORLD WAR II

1. *Attucks: The School That Opened a City* (documentary file, dir. Ted Green; Ted Green films, 2016).

2. John Morton-Finney Papers, Black History News & Notes, Indiana Historical Society, box 20, folder 3, number 99, 2005.

3. Harry W. Brooks Papers, Manuscript and Visual Collections, Indiana Historical Society.

4. *Attucks: The School That Opened a City.*

5. Brigadier General Norris W. Overton, United States Airforce Archives, May 1981.

6. American Battle Monument Commission, *Origins of the Tuskegee Airmen-99th Fighter Squadron: First Encounters with Enemy Aircraft* (Arlington, VA: American Battle Monument Commission, 2018).

7. Charles Barclay Hall Jr., interview by the author, July 15, 2019.

8. American Legion, Tinker Air Force Base Publication.

9. Michele Obama, Tuskegee University Commencement, 2016, in *Attucks: The School That Opened a City.*

10. Charles DeBow, *I Got Wings: An Autobiographical Account of One of the Original Tuskegee Airmen* (National Black Chamber of Commerce, 2020); *Indianapolis Recorder,* February 27, 1982.

11. Stanley Sandler, *Segregated Skies: All Black Squadron of World War II* (Washington, DC: Smithsonian Institution Press, 1993); "Charles DeBow," *Life,* March 1942.

12. "Graham Edward Martin, Member of the Golden Thirteen," United States Naval Institute, Annapolis, Maryland, oral history.

13. "Graham Edward Martin," United States Naval Institute.

14. "Graham Edward Martin," United States Naval Institute.

15. "Graham Edward Martin," United States Naval Institute.

16. Paul Stillwell, *The Golden Thirteen: Recollections of the First Black Naval Officers* (Naval Institute Press, 1993); Elayne Martin-Lewis, interview, August 28, 2020.

17. Paul Stillwell, "A Step Forward," *Naval History Blog,* United States Naval Institute, February 12, 2019, https://www.navalhistory.org/2019/02/12/a-step-forward.

18. DeAnne Blanton, "Women Soldiers of the Civil War," *Prologue* 25, no. 1, 1993.

19. Philip Thomas Tucker, *Cathay Williams: From Slave to Female Buffalo Soldier* (Mechanicsburg, PA: Stackpole, 2009).

20. Alberta Stanley-White, *Sister Soldier Network: The Story—The Resource—The Spirit—Telling Our Story Our Way,* November 19, 2017.

21. Alberta Stanley-White, interview by the author, June 20, 2018.

22. Melton A. McLaurin, *The Marines of Montford Point: America's First Black Marines* (Chapel Hill: University of North Carolina Press, 2007).

23. Ellen Price-Lane, interview by the author, February 24, 2020.

24. David Leander Williams, *Indianapolis Jazz: The Masters, Legends and Legacy of Indiana Avenue* (Charleston, SC: History Press, 2014), 165–67.

19. THE 1950S

1. *Attucks: The School That Opened a City* (documentary file, dir. Ted Green; Ted Green films, 2016).

2. Oscar Robertson, "Monument Circle Incident," *Indianapolis Recorder*, April 4, 1955.

3. Robertson, "Monument Circle Incident."

4. Municipal Record Books of Pittsfield, Massachusetts, 33:573–74.

5. Alan J. Pollock, *Barnstorming to Heaven: Syd Pollock and His Great Black Teams* (Tuscaloosa: University of Alabama Press, 2006), 1–3.

6. Clifford Robinson, interview by the author, June 14, 2019.

7. Robinson, interview.

8. Pollock, *Barnstorming to Heaven*, 10–13.

9. Robinson, interview.

10. Robinson, interview.

11. Robinson, interview.

20. THE ENTERTAINMENT INDUSTRY FLEXES ITS MUSCLE

1. "Negroes Not Barred from Riverside Park," *Indianapolis Recorder*, August 30, 1958.

2. David J. Bodenhamer and Robert G. Barrows, *Encyclopedia of Indianapolis* (Bloomington: Indiana University Press, 1994), 45–46.

3. Tiffany Benedict Browne, "Back Tract: Riverside Amusement Park," *Indianapolis Monthly*, June 26, 2016.

4. Flo Garvin, interview by the author, April 15, 2002

5. Flo Garvin, interview by the author, July 22, 2002.

6. "Turf Club Owner Unmoved," *Indianapolis Recorder*, March 12, 1960.

7. "Turf Club Owner Unmoved," *Indianapolis Recorder*.

8. David Leander Williams, "Taking Jimi Hendrix to School," *Indianapolis Eye Electronic Newspaper*, June 30, 2003.

9. David Leander Williams, *Indianapolis Jazz: The Masters, Legends and Legacy of Indiana Avenue* (Charleston, SC: History Press, 2014), 194.

10. Tom Ridley, interview by the author, July 4, 2019.

21. THE BLACK COMMUNITY BATTLES NEGATIVE STEREOTYPES AND INTRODUCES JAZZ AND POETRY

1. David J. Bodenhamer and Robert G. Barrows, "Early Television Stations," *Encyclopedia of Indianapolis* (Bloomington: Indiana University Press, 1994), 15–16, 19.

2. "Milton Berle Television Show," *Indianapolis Recorder*, November 12, 1955.

3. Elizabeth McLeod, *The Original Amos 'n' Andy, Freeman Gosden and Charles Correll* (Jefferson, NC: McFarland).

4. David Leander Williams, *Indianapolis Jazz: The Masters, Legends and Legacy of Indiana Avenue* (Charleston, SC: History Press, 2014), 188, 190.

5. Williams, *Indianapolis Jazz*, 86.

6. Williams, *Indianapolis Jazz*, 87.

7. Williams, *Indianapolis Jazz*, 89.

8. Williams, *Indianapolis Jazz*, 82.

9. Joshua Berrett and Louis Bourgois III, *The Musical World of J. J. Johnson* (Lanham, MD: Scarecrow, 1999), 99–100.

10. "At Home with J. J. David Whiteis," *Downbeat*, April 1995, 26.

11. Williams, *Indianapolis Jazz*, 84.

12. Williams, *Indianapolis Jazz*.

13. Mari Evans, interview, June 24, 2014.

22. THE INDIANA AVENUE JAZZ CONNECTION/CRISPUS ATTUCKS/McARTHUR CONSERVATORY/THE EXODUS

1. David Leander Williams, *Indianapolis Jazz: The Masters, Legends and Legacy of Indiana Avenue* (Charleston, SC: History Press, 2014), 140.

2. Williams, *Indianapolis Jazz*, 141.

3. Williams, *Indianapolis Jazz*, 138.

4. Williams, *Indianapolis Jazz*, 147.

5. Williams, *Indianapolis Jazz*, 148.

6. Williams, *Indianapolis Jazz*, 148.

7. *Jazz Showcase: Introducing the Master Sounds* (Hollywood, CA: World Pacific Records, 1957).

8. *Jazz Showcase: Introducing the Master Sounds.*

9. *Jazz Showcase: Introducing the Master Sounds.*

10. Steve Cerra, "Remembering the Mastersounds," *Jazz Profiles* (blog), July 21, 2020, https://jazzprofiles.blogspot.com/2020/07/remembering-mastersounds.html.

23. HISTORIC FIRSTS OF THE 1960s AND THEIR MOVERS AND SHAKERS

1. David J. Bodenhamer and Robert G. Barrows, *Encyclopedia of Indianapolis* (Bloomington: Indiana University Press, 1994), 748–49.

2. "Longest Survivor of Implant Dead," *New York Times*, November 28, 1974, 23.

3. Bodenhamer and Barrows, "F. B. Ransom," *Encyclopedia of Indianapolis*, 1165–66.

4. Judith Ransom-Lewis, interview by the author, June 20, 2018.

5. "Dr. Joseph H. Ward," *Freeman*, July 22, 1899.

6. Clara Merritt DeBoer, *Blacks and the American Missionary Association* (Bristol, TN: United Church of Christ, 1973).

7. Michelle D. Hale, "Robert L. Bailey," *Encyclopedia of Indianapolis*, 288.

8. Flanner House Records, Ruth Lilly Special Collections and Archives, Indiana University–Purdue University at Indianapolis.

9. Flanner House Records, Ruth Lilly Special Collections and Archives, Indiana University–Purdue University at Indianapolis.

10. "Pioneers in Black History," *Indianapolis Star,* February 15, 2015.

11. Naomii Brack, "Rufus Calvin Kuykendall (1903–1977)," *Black Past,* November 15, 2020, https://www.blackpast.org/african-american-history/people-african-american-history/rufus-calvin-kuykendall-1903-1977/.

12. Stuart Mortuary Obituary, *Obsequies for the Honorable Mercer Montgomery Mance,* Monday, October 22, 1990.

13. Carole Boston Weatherford, *Freedom on the Menu: The Greensboro Sit-Ins* (New York: Penguin, 2007).

14. "Tension in Alabama," *Indianapolis Recorder,* June 15, 1963.

15. "Church Blast 'Mars' 'Love That Forgives,'" *Indianapolis Recorder,* September 21, 1965.

16. Robert E. Boomhower, *Robert F. Kennedy and the 1968 Indiana Primary* (Bloomington: Indiana University Press, 2008), 2, 6.

17. *Indianapolis Recorder,* June 6, 1933.

18. Bodenhamer and Barrows, "Brokenburr," *Encyclopedia of Indianapolis,* 357.

19. Andrew Ramsey, "Faburn DeFrantz," *Indianapolis Recorder,* October 3, 1964.

20. Bodenhamer and Barrows, "DeFrantz," *Encyclopedia of Indianapolis,* 496.

21. Bodenhamer and Barrows, "Henry J. Richardson," *Encyclopedia of Indianapolis,* 1194.

22. "Voice from the Gallery: Chief DeFrantz like Moses," *Indianapolis Recorder,* October 3, 1964.

23. Joseph Ramsey, interview by the author, September 13, 2020.

24. Funeral obituary, Dr. Andrew Johnny Brown, Cherished Song: "I'll Fly Away," Stuart Mortuary, August 1996.

25. Reverend Thomas Brown, interview by the author, June 30, 2019.

26. A'Lelia Bundles, interview by the author, May 1, 2019.

27. Hallie Bryant, interview by the author, June 19, 2020.

28. John Dumas-Haamid, interview by the author, July 5, 2018.

29. A'Lelia Perry Bundles, interview by the author, S. Henry Bundles Memoir.

30. A'Lelia Bundles, interview by the author, May 1, 2019.

31. A'Lelia Perry Bundles, family archives.

24. WOMEN OF VALOR

1. "Everyday People: Harriette Bailey Conn," *Traces of Indiana and Midwestern History* (2008): 30.

2. Ray Boomhower, *The Lady in the Hat: Mattie Coney and Citizens Forum, Indiana Historical Society Blog,* November 20, 2020, https://indianahistory.org/blog/the-lady-in-the-hat-mattie-coney-and-citizens-forum/.

3. "Carson Remembered: Congresswoman Gave Voice to the Disadvantaged," *Indianapolis Star*, December 19, 2007.

4. "She Fought Racial Barriers—Noble Woman Roselyn Richardson," *Indianapolis News*, July 31, 1979.

5. "She Fought Racial Barriers," *Indianapolis News*.

6. "She Fought Racial Barriers," *Indianapolis News*.

7. Roselyn Comer Richardson Obituary, *Indianapolis Star*, July 12, 2005.

8. Osma D. Spurlock Obituary, *Indianapolis Star*, April 18, 2007.

25. URBAN RENEWAL IS NEGRO REMOVAL

1. David J. Bodenhamer and Robert G. Barrows, *Encyclopedia of Indianapolis* (Bloomington: Indiana University Press, 1994), 362–63.

2. Nicole Poletika, "The Undemocratic Making of Indianapolis," *Belt Magazine*, March 29, 2019.

3. Fred Ramos and Steve Hammer, "The Death of a Black Neighborhood: It's a Lot Different Now Along Indiana Avenue," *NUVO Newsweekly*, July 20–27, 1994.

4. *Indianapolis Recorder*, May 1, 1971.

5. James Glass, "A Historical Look at Indianapolis' I-65/70 Split," *Indianapolis Star*, May 1, 1971.

6. Richard Ellis, interviewed by Gerald Hause, July 18, 2019.

7. Albert Coleman, interview by the author, March 17, 2020.

8. Albert Coleman, interview by the author, March 17, 2020.

BIBLIOGRAPHY

Badger, Reid. *A Life in Ragtime: A Biography of James Reese Europe.* New York: Oxford University Press, 1995.

Balf, Todd. *Major: A Black Athlete, a White Era, and the Fight to Be the World's Fastest Human Being.* New York: Crown, 2008.

Bodenhamer, David J., and Robert G. Barrows. *Encyclopedia of Indianapolis.* Bloomington: Indiana University Press, 1994.

Brady, Carolyn M. "Indianapolis at the Time of the Great Migration, 1900–1920." *Black History News & Notes,* no. 65, August 1996.

Bundles, A'Lelia. *Madam C. J. Walker, Entrepreneur.* New York: Chelsea House, 1991.

———. *On Her Own Ground: The Life and Times of Madam C. J. Walker.* New York: Scribner, 2001.

Carroll, Joseph Cephas. *Slave Insurrections in the United States, 1800–1865.* Mineola, NY: Dover, 2004.

Cave, Alfred A. *The French and Indian War.* Westport, CT: Greenwood, 2004.

Cockrum, William M. *Pioneer History of Indiana.* Oakland City, IN: Press of Oakland City Journal, 1907.

Crenshaw, Gwendolyn. *Bury Me in a Free Land.* Indianapolis: Indiana Historical Bureau, 1986.

Eagle, Bob, and Eric S. LeBlanc. *Blues: A Regional Experience.* Santa Barbara, CA: Praeger, 2013.

Esarey, Logan. *A History of Indiana from Its Exploration to 1850.* Indianapolis: B. F. Bowen, 1918.

Ferguson, Earline Rae. "African-Americans Women's Club Work: A Community Affair." PhD diss., Indiana University, 1997.

Gale, Frederick. *A Biographical Study of Persons for Whom Indianapolis Public Schools Are Named.* Indianapolis: Indianapolis Public Schools Public Relations Department, 1965.

Gould, Todd. *Gold and Glory: Charlie Wiggins and the African-American Racing Car Circuit.* Bloomington: Indiana University Press, 2002.

Hawk, Madgelyn. *When the Mourning Dove Cries.* Self-published, Authorhouse, 2003.

Hicks, Luther C. *Great Black Hoosier Americans.* Indianapolis: Luther Hicks, 1977.

Labode, Modupe. "A 'Voice from the Gallery': Andrew Ramsey and School Desegregation in Indianapolis." *Ohio Valley History* 14, no. 3 (Fall 2014): 26–48.

Minton, Linda E. *Remembering World War II Women.* Self-published, 2018.

Montell, William Lynwood. *The Saga of Coe Ridge: A Study in Oral History.* New York: Harper and Row, 1970.

Payne, Patricia, and Annmarie Byers. *An African-American Experience: The Negro Baseball Leagues.* Indianapolis: Office of African-Centered/Multicultural Education, Indianapolis Public Schools, 1995.

Peters, Pamela R. *The Underground Railroad in Floyd County, Indiana.* Jefferson, NC: McFarland, 2001.

Petry, Ashley. *Indianapolis: A Guide to the Weird, Wonderful, and Obscure.* St. Louis, MO: Reedy Press, 2019.

Pollock, Alan J. *Barnstorming to Heaven: Syd Pollock and His Great Black Teams.* Tuscaloosa: University of Alabama Press, 2006.

Power-Greene, Ousmane K. *Against the Wind and Tide: The African-American Struggle against the Colonization Movement.* New York: New York University Press, 2014.

Ridley, Thomas. *From the Avenue: A Memoir.* Indianapolis: self-published, 2012.

Ritchie, Andrew. *Major Taylor: The Fastest Bicycle Rider in the World.* San Francisco: Van Der Plas, 1988.

Sandler, Stanley. *Segregated Skies: All Black Squadron of World War II.* Washington, DC: Smithsonian Institution Press, 1993.

Starms, Robert W. *Achieving Christian Social Goals through the Public Forum: An Interpretative Study of the Monster Meeting.* Indianapolis: Senate Avenue YMCA, 1944.

Stillwell, Paul. *The Golden Thirteen: Recollection of the First Black Naval Officers.* Annapolis, MD: Naval Institute Press, 1993.

Thornbrough, Emma Lou. *The Negro in Indiana before 1900: A Study of a Minority.* Bloomington: Indiana University Press, 1993.

———. *This Far by Faith: Black Hoosier Heritage.* Indianapolis: Indiana Committee for the Humanities, Indiana Historical Society, 1982.

Warren, Stanley. *Crispus Attucks High School: Hail to the Green, Hail to the Gold.* Virginia Beach, VA: Donning, 1998.

———. "The Monster Meetings at the Negro Y.M.C.A. in Indianapolis." *Indiana Magazine of History* XCI, no. 1 (March 1995): 57–80.

Washington, Booker T. *Up from Slavery: An Autobiography.* New York: Double Day, 1901.

Williams, David Leander. "The Ferguson Brothers and Indiana Avenue." *Traces of Indiana and Midwestern History* 19, no. 3 (Summer 2007): 36–39.

———. *Indianapolis Jazz: The Masters, Legends and Legacy of Indiana Avenue.* Charleston, SC: History Press, 2014.

Yenser, Thomas. *Who's Who in Colored America.* Brooklyn, NY: Thomas Yenser, 1937.

INDEX

DAVID L. WILLIAMS is author of *Indianapolis African-American History, Indianapolis Jazz: The Masters, Legends and Legacy of Indiana Avenue,* and *Indianapolis Rhythm and Blues.* He has also written articles dealing with Indianapolis African American history for *African Americans in Indianapolis* and *Traces of Indiana and Midwestern History,* a magazine from the Indiana Historical Society. In his free time Williams collects memorabilia, historical artifacts, and information about African American history, particularly slavery and African American music history. Williams received his Bachelor of Arts degree from Colorado State University and his Master of Arts degree from Fairleigh Dickinson University. He is currently based in Indianapolis, Indiana.